"The survival stories in this book will touch your heart in a special way, and inspire you to rise higher."
— **Laurel Winston, author of** *Carrots Grow from Carrot Seeds: Cultivating 21st Century Customer Service*

"In *Evolving Through Adversity*, we gain a wealth of knowledge about a country and a culture we would not otherwise know, and I'm grateful for Ms. Nimenya for sharing her story."
— **Brenda Milewski, author of** *Evolving Your Leadership Style: It's Not Rocket Science*

"Overcoming obstacles is a lesson anyone can benefit from. In this book, the author narrates her experiences, so that you too, can learn and overcome."
— **Carol Paul, author of** *Team Clean: The Ultimate Family Clean-Up-The House Formula*

"Seconde, I enjoyed your book, and I will make sure everyone I know reads it. So many insights, so much wisdom you share. Thank you."
— **Bonnie Richter, Vice-President of Winners Don't Quit Association**

D1396798

Dear Bonnie,
Thank you for giving a voice
to the voiceless.

Love & Peace
Praise for *Seconde*
EVOLVING THROUGH ADVERSITY

"This book is great and so inspiring. I can't even imagine moving halfway across the world and readjusting to a new culture. I really enjoyed reading *Evolving Through Adversity*."
— **Tyler R. Tichelaar, Ph.D. and award-winning author of**
The Best Place

"If you are looking for a resource to give you hope and for overcoming all life's adversities, then, start here!"
— **Patrick Snow, international best-selling author of**
Creating Your Own Destiny **and** *The Affluent Entrepreneur*

"What a gift! Written by an extraordinary woman who, through much adversity, finds incredible potential within herself. This book is filled with lessons of perseverance and hope, beneficial to everyone."
— **Susan Friedmann, CSP, international best-selling author of**
Riches in Niches: How to Make it BIG in a small Market

"Growing up in a culture completely unlike our own, we learn about the experiences of a little girl whose pain and history shaped her into who she is today."
— **H.C. "Joe" Raymond, author of** *Embracing Change from the Inside Out*

"Seconde Nimenya's *Evolving Through Adversity* is a personal testament of courage and hope. It is a must read for those interested in personal evolution and cultural change."
— **Robin B. O'Grady, author of** *The Optimist's Edge: Moving Beyond Negativism to Create Your Amazing Life*

"*Evolving Through Adversity* is an example of how we can't love and honor others, without first loving and honoring ourselves. Love comes from within, and this book teaches us how to find it."
— **B. Imei Hsu, LMHC and Founding Counselor of Seattle Direct Counseling**

"In *Evolving Through Adversity*, we learn about other cultures different from ours, and how as individuals, we can all evolve past adversity."
— **Bruce Raine, author of** *Attitude Determines Destiny: Experience a Better Day Everyday*

"I wish such a book had been written a long time ago, but everything comes when we're ready for it to transform our lives for the better."
— **Frank Reed, author of** *In God We Trust, Dollar$ & Sense*

"This book is one of a kind and will change lives in a greater way than you could have imagined. I truly believe God used Seconde's voice to speak to mankind. It's about time we join forces and build strong families."
— **Mary West, author of** *Networking Your Way To Wealth*

"I love learning about other cultures, so I found Seconde's story very fascinating, and uplifting all at once. This is a valuable resource for people to assess their obstacles and then discover and honor their true selves."
— **Terry Gargus, M.S., author of** *Reinventing Any Life*

A LEADERSHIP ROADMAP TO EMBRACING CHANGE

EVOLVING THROUGH ADVERSITY

How to Overcome Obstacles,
Discover Your Passion
and Honor Your True Self

SECONDE NIMENYA

Address all inquiries to:
Seconde Nimenya
Tel: 425-213-8606
Email: nisecond@gmail.com
www.evolvingthroughadversity.com

Published by Aviva Publishing
Lake Placid, NY 12946
Phone: 518-523-1320
www.avivapubs.com

Edited by Tyler Tichelaar
Cover & Interior Design by Fusion Creative Works
Author Photo by Sandra Hixson-Matthews.

Library of Congress Control Number: 2013941005
Nimenya, Seconde.
Evolving Through Adversity: how to overcome obstacles, discover your passion, and honor your true self / Seconde Nimenya.

Print ISBN: 978-1-938686-59-7
Overcoming – memoir.   I. Title.
Finding purpose –self-help   3. Education   4. Family.   5. Relationships
II. Title.

First Edition

Printed in the United States of America

For book orders visit: www.evolvingthroughadversity.com

DEDICATION

To my maternal grandmother whose angelic and loving spirit continued to sustain me long after she was gone.

To my parents, Suzanne and Gaspard: I dedicate this book to you. You sure gave me a life full of writing material; I love you and want to honor you.

To my husband, Claver: forgiving each other wasn't easy, but it was worth it. Thank you for another shot at loving you.

To my precious children: Carmelle, Elva, and Darrel, for your unconditional love and your patience. I know it hasn't been easy for you being brought up with a dichotomy of cultures and traditions, not to mention your parents' English accent! I am very fortunate to have you as my children and I thank you for picking me to be your mommy. I hope I didn't mess you up too much, and I ask for your forgiveness if I have. You are wonderful, intelligent, funny, and beautiful; never let anyone tell you that you're not. Stay true to who you are and honor yourselves. I love you.

To my uncles: Vincent and Apollinaire. Without you, I wouldn't know how to read or write; and I certainly wouldn't have written this book. You paid for my elementary and high school education, giving me the gift that keeps on giving. Thank you so very much.

And to you dear reader: May my stories uplift you and help you discover and honor your true self.

With much love,

Seconde Nimenya

CONTENTS

FOREWORD

Growing up in the United States in a loving middle income family, I was sheltered from a lot of the adversity that many less-fortunate children experience daily. Our family was blessed always to have lots of food, and love in our home.

As I grew older, started to travel around the world, and welcome friends from other cultures, I soon learned that many of the things I took for granted as a child were not accessible to most children. What I discovered through this awakening was that some of the most talented, successful, and hard- working people I know came from a youth full of adversity, uncertainty, and doing without. What I learned was the truth behind Nietzsche's quote: "That which does not kill us makes us stronger."

More times than not, those who grow up unprivileged learn at an early age the importance of hard work, determination, and never giving up. Successful people have learned how to embrace change and take a leadership role in their lives. They learned at an early age, "If it is to be, it is up to me."

In this powerful book by Seconde Nimenya, you will learn what it truly means to evolve as a human being, as a result of facing and overcoming all the events that occur in your life. You will learn that you are stronger than you could have imagined, and you have the strength to persevere in any and all hardship.

In *Evolving Through Adversity*, Seconde shares with you her life story of growing up in Burundi (Central Africa). At one time during her childhood, due to a civil war, Seconde's family was broken up and scattered throughout the country, hiding in the bushes and mountains to avoid gun- fires and machetes. Seconde did not know whether she and her family would live or whether she would ever see her family reunited. Due to subsequent civil wars in her motherland, Seconde chose a life in North America so she could raise her family in a more peaceful country, and provide stability and opportunity to her children.

Throughout this book, you will walk a lifetime in her shoes, and as a result of doing so, you will learn to appreciate better the many blessings in your life. In each chapter, you'll be asked to answer many of Seconde's evolving questions for reflection, so you, too, can learn from Seconde's story, how to overcome obstacles, discover your passion, and honor your true self.

You'll learn how to acquire the specific knowledge and skills needed to overcome all adversity that enters into your path. Furthermore, you'll learn to take a greater leadership role in your life, embrace change, and focus on the things in life that you're blessed with, instead of being obsessed with what you do not have. As a result, you will attain happiness in your life by learning how to honor your true self.

So, get ready for an exciting journey that encompasses two continents, a multitude of cultures, and numerous strategies to help you evolve into the leader you were meant to be. Buckle your seat-belt and get ready for a life-changing experience. You may never be the same again!

Patrick Snow
International Best-Selling Author of *Creating Your Own Destiny* and *The Affluent Entrepreneur*
www.PatrickSnow.com

Introduction

CONQUERING
MY EMOTIONS

*Anyone who survived childhood has enough material to write
for the rest of his or her life.*
— Flannery O'Connor

I first read the above quote in Anne Lamott's *Bird by Bird: Some
Instructions on Writing and Life,* a book our writing instructor Nick
O'Connell assigned us when I took my writing class in Seattle. This
passage struck me because I was feeling a little insecure about sharing my own childhood survival stories, but I decided that maybe—
just maybe—my story was worth telling.

This book explores my life journey, my efforts to fit in, and the
different guardian angels who have crossed my path along the way.
It is not meant to teach politics or history. If I happen to talk about
people, historical events or facts, it is to reminisce on those events
because they impacted my life directly or indirectly in that time
and place, and to the best of my recollection. Distances are an estimate in equivalent miles. I use real names when talking about
my family members, but in some cases, I've changed or withheld
names of some people to protect their privacy.

After reading this book, my hope is that you will feel uplifted. I intend it to carry a message of awareness, peace, nurturance, love, harmony, and forgiveness in our families, our communities, our countries, and our world. This is a story of breaking free from beliefs I no longer hold, and resilience by accepting and honoring who I am.

This story evolved from several emotional journals I have kept over the years. Sometimes, the emotional journals were my best friends where I could expose my feelings without shame or interruption. Some days, I would feel emotionally heavy and write something in my journal while my eyes would be blurred by tears. What I love about journaling your feelings is that you don't have to edit them for appropriateness. You just dive in with a pen, and pour your heart on the paper. It feels so good afterwards that you think, "What was I so sad about? Or why was I so angry?" Journaling your feelings gives you clarity, and you can make sound decisions after. It's a type of meditation (or even cheap therapy!) where you take a break and can make conscious choices afterward. Journaling is a coping mechanism that can help you deal with whatever is at hand—whether it's a difficult decision you have to make or you just have to get the negative emotions out of your system, so no one gets hurt.

My intention is to inspire you to rise above your circumstances, whatever they may be, so you can thrive by discovering who you are and honoring your true self. Maybe life has given you lemons, but you didn't always know how to make lemonade. We all have things to battle in this life, some small, some big. And we all cope differently—some well, some not so well. Let's learn from each other.

Are you ready to begin honoring your true self? Can we take this life journey together? Do you have an open mind? I will hold your hand and you will hold mine; I want us to mentor each other and help each other grow. Don't spend another day living with a heavy load on your shoulders. Let's go to the school of life together.

RRU MODEL — REFLECT

RRU MODEL — RECTIFY

RRU MODEL — UNITE

Part 1: Africa

THE EARLY YEARS

Chapter 1

RISING FROM THE ASHES

You know the only people who are always sure about the proper way to raise children? Those who've never had any.
— Bill Cosby

Once upon a time, when I was still in a crawling stage, I was home alone with my mother. It was lunch-time, and she was preparing food for our family, some corn dough that we call *ubugali* (or *ugali* in Swahili*)*. It is a staple in many parts of Burundi, especially in the high plateau. It goes well with beef stew or just beans mixed with green leafy vegetables, the latter being more affordable.

My mother momentarily left the area where there was a live cooking fire and boiling water, to get the flour in another room, leaving me, the crawling baby, in charge. I crawled after her, obviously not wanting to be left alone. I took the short-cut in her direction, tripping and falling into her pot, three-quarters full of boiling water, which in turn spilled into the live fire, creating enough smoke to burst all smoke alarms (but we had none). And I, the crawling baby, dipped the entire left side of my body: face, arm, leg—into the gleaming fire now doused into hot ashes, thereby burning my small body. I don't know how long I was in those hot ashes, but when my mother returned with her corn flour, she found me grilling to the bone. I can imagine the awful guilt my mom felt when she realized she should have known better than to leave a crawling baby beside a live fire and boiling water.

I was immediately (I hope) rushed to the nearest hospital, about an hour's drive under normal traffic and road conditions, but my parents had no car. They had to walk to that hospital. I learned from my older siblings that my burn was very bad. I was at the hospital close to a year. But time did a good job, and I am happy to report that I fully recovered from the burn trauma and injury. I know I fought for my life with my left hand because that is where I still have scars after all these years. I don't think those scars will ever disappear—a sign forever of how close I came to death. God really spared me that day.

Immediately following my release from the hospital, my mother took me to her parents. Although my stay there was supposed to be temporary, I lived with my maternal grandparents until I finished primary school. In any case, it was like a tradition because all my siblings, except my oldest sister Eugenie, were sent to stay with my grandparents on my mom's side, but only short-term. Only my second oldest sister, Claire, lived there until sixth grade. My two older brothers, Emmanuel and Cyriaque, stayed there a short time and went back to live with my parents when it was time to start school. And here I was, the fifth child. It was my turn to live with Grandpa Bunyoni and my beloved grandmother, Biragumye.

When my grandparents took me in, I was very small and fragile to say the least. When one day, one of my grandmother's best friends saw me, she told her, "My dear friend, although you have been taking care of your daughter's kids, this one is going to be an exception." She implied that I would not make it. My grandmother's feelings were hurt, but Grandma never held a grudge;

they remained best friends as long as I can remember. Her friend was like a second grandmother to me, although she wasn't as loving as my beloved Grandmother (*Nyogokuru* in Kirundi). Grandma made it her goal that she would return me to my parents in better shape than she had received me.

Needless to say my grandparents were poor. But since there wasn't any calculated poverty line or threshold at that time, it seemed that poverty wasn't even a word very much known in the villages. My grandmother and my aunts, who lived at home at the time always managed to have something to fill our stomachs. I ate food we grew and I drank fresh banana juice made from the bananas grown on my grandparents' farm. Unless Mother Nature was angry and provided too much or too little rain, we had enough food. At home, I sometimes wore my aunt Aurelia's oversized shirts, which became dresses for me; and on the first day of school when I started first grade, I wore borrowed clothes from a neighbor's child. So as long as I didn't go without eating for a day, we weren't really poor.

In addition, my grandfather had nearly a hundred cows from when my grandparents first moved to the southern region from the highlands of Bururi province. The southern regions had caused many cattle owners to migrate because they sought greener pastures, which were in abundance in the lower lands and valleys of the country still uninhabited. However, by the time I turned nine or ten years old, we had less than ten cows left. Even though there was rich grass in the lower south, cows didn't tolerate well the summer's heat and humidity. Also, there were too many bugs compared to the hilly landscapes. Therefore, my grandfather's hundred cows had dwindled to ten. Each time a cow was sick, numerous traditional medicines were sought. All of my grandfather's attention was oriented toward his cows. My grandmother did her best to get the cow medicine, which consisted of herbs and other leaves. She tried different kinds to get the cure, but sometimes, she couldn't find the right combination, or she would find it when it was already too late for the cow.

Although life was not easy, we had everything, or I had everything. I had grandparents who loved me unconditionally, cows that filled our compound, and baby cows that occupied half of our house. We had cats too, lots of them. I didn't like them because they slept in my bed, and sometimes, they had babies right there in the corner beside my bed. We didn't know that they triggered my grandmother's asthma attacks. I only have this knowledge now. When I look back, I remember that my grandmother never had a reprieve from her asthma. And since there was a lot of milk, cats always were there, drinking my milk. I didn't like milk, so that was okay—the cats were welcome to drink it all. Grandma tried to force me to drink warm milk fresh out of the cow, but I couldn't. I would take it, go in hiding, and spill it on the dusty floor or in the kitties' milk container. Once in a while, I would drink skim milk.

Skimming, to separate milk from cream, was an elaborate process that used a churn, called *igisabo* in Kirundi. You put milk into the churn, and in a circle motion, you agitated it for about an hour or until the butter granules formed that needed to be separated from the milk. Then you drained the milk into a different container and put the butter in another.

Aging the butter was also a long process that consisted of putting it in a cool dry place in a covered container, and leaving it for months without touching it. When it was considered ripened enough, I remember my grandmother would put a small slice of butter in the food as a condiment; it would melt in, and it was actually yummy! That was the only type of butter my grandmother allowed herself to consume. Because of her health issues, Grandma had limited food choices. So, we used this butter quite often, and my grandfather preferred cow butter to the palm oil that we only used rarely.

At my grandparents' house, my daily chores consisted of fetching cooking wood, carrying water from the river (three miles away), and when I was old enough, leading the cows to the pastures. Once, one of our cows taught me an important lesson about daydreaming. I must have been on cloud nine when I found myself on top of the cow's horns and up in the air. Usually, when a cow picks you up like that, it shakes you in circular motions and then throws you at a distance. I was afraid of calling for help because I didn't want to make the cow more nervous. Fortunately, before the cow started shaking me on its long horns, a neighbor, who was herding his cows in the same pasture, saw the scene and rushed to save me from the cow. Seeing him come toward it, the cow bent its head and dropped me on the ground. I landed with only minor injuries. That day, I hated cows! I wished them all to be slaughtered right away, so we could eat their meat, and I would be freed from leading them to the pastures. But, of course, no matter what the cows did, my grandfather wasn't going to let that happen. And it's not what I wanted either. If nothing else, I liked our cows for filling our property; they gave me a sense of security, as if the cows were our security guards.

That special cow was a tough one. I remember one time cow thieves came to my grandparents' farm in the night and stole all our cows, except that one. It had chased them away, and it even woke my grandparents by running around, making noises, pushing the fence, and knocking on the house's door with its horns. That's how we found out that all the cows were gone, except that one. My grandparents called out to neighbors to help and followed in the cows' footprints. Five miles away, the thieves heard the people following in their tracks and calling out, so they gave up and ran into hiding. My grandparents were able to bring our cows back home. It was the scariest night of my youth. Back then, stealing cows was the ultimate threat against cattle owners. Many cattle thieves did it as a lucrative business, and they attempted to steal my grandfather's cows many more times, but the tough cow always chased them away. Sometimes, they would bring salt to tempt the cows to follow them because cows crave salt. But the tough one always kicked them away until eventually they gave up. We named that cow *Bihayi,* "glory".

After my incident with our proud cow Bihayi, I was released from cow herding, leaving that chore to Barenga, my adopted aunt (she had been adopted by my grandparents as a child). My grandma preferred to send me to fetch water and firewood. I liked fetching water better because I could meet other kids my age at the river and play in the water, getting myself wet from head to toe while trying to catch tadpoles. Some of the older girls said that if you got a tadpole to bite your nipples, your breasts would grow instantly. Some of my friends had started growing boobs by then, but I still had a flat chest. So I needed all the help I could get. Despite my efforts, I never caught a tadpole; they're the fastest thing in water.

Some days, I took so long before I brought the water home that my grandma got mad at me because she needed water to start cooking dinner, especially when she was making dry beans that took hours to cook. Because she was unable to pronounce my name correctly, she called me Sakunda instead. "Sakunda, where were you all this time…? Where were you child?" she would demand each time I came back with a bucket half-full of water because I had spilled it all the way home from the river as I tried to rush. She would only yell at me, and she was never upset for more than a minute, letting my grandfather be the bad cop.

Whenever I misbehaved, my grandfather chased me with his walker and hit me with it on my behind, my legs, or even on my head if it were what he could reach. I drove him crazy by running from him and hiding. "Child, come back here! Soon or later I will get you!" Grandpa would threaten because my hiding would work up his anger. And until he had given me a good correction, he never let go. Unlike Grandma, he never let me get away with anything. Even when I hid from him for a day, he would still punish me when I resurfaced. And whenever my grandfather started whipping my behind, my grandmother would defend me, telling him to stop. "Bunyoni, leave that child alone; what will I tell her mother? She entrusted us with that child!" Grandma would say between coughs due to her chronic asthma.

"You tell her that you spoil this child rotten. That's what you will tell her mother or I will!" Grandpa would say.

Although my grandparents never knew it, I was terrified that they would tell my mother I was misbehaving when she would visit us. I prayed that they would forget to tell her about my mischief. And since they were old, I expected them to forget. The idea of telling my mother on me sounded like a way to make me do penance. I had heard my big sister Claire talk about my mother's disciplinarian methods. In those days, hitting a child wasn't considered child abuse; it was tough love. At times, only corporal punishment could reach me and make me behave. Now as a parent myself, I realize that since my grandmother didn't punish me that much, I needed that balance my grandpa provided.

Despite his harsh disciplining, Grandpa loved me, and I still have sweet memories of him. He always gave me leftovers from his food, even when I was full and he wasn't; it was an affectionate gesture, a sign of his love. He was also my favorite story-teller at bedtime. He told me stories of the big-headed monster (*igisizimwe*) that always chased ill-behaved children. The stories didn't actually put me to sleep; they scared me to death and kept me up at night. So, the next day, I would try to behave to avoid meeting the terrifying creature. Grandpa also taught me to pay attention to worldwide news from an early age. He believed that happenings in other parts of the world affected us even in our remote village. He was a news consumer, listening to the radio that his son, my uncle Apollinaire, had given us. And today, knowing what's happening elsewhere in the world keeps me grounded; I attribute that gift to my grandfather.

When my grandparents got older and less mobile, punishment was left mostly to my aunt Aurelia before she got married. She wasn't much of a hitter, but one day, she gave me the lesson of my young life. I was in third grade, and with my best friend Seraphine and my maternal cousin Mediatrice, we started fooling around and getting to school first an hour late, then two hours late. We would leave home early in the mornings, meet up at our meeting place, and walk slowly, talking and playing games so that we forgot we were going to school. After two or three days of this routine, we eventually started not showing up at all. One day, we were so late that we saw students coming back home after school while we were still on our way. We then turned back and headed home as if we had been in school. Our parents never suspected what we were up to, until a week later when the school summoned them to come and meet our principal and our respective teachers. When the summons was sent home, I instantly knew I was in big trouble. Although Mediatrice and Seraphine were also in trouble, I was the only one not leaving with my "real" parents. I knew that whatever punishment I was in for would be doubled once my mother heard about what I had done.

Aunt Aurelia answered the summons and took me to school that day. After she had been briefed on my case, she went in the nearby bush, cut a fresh switch off a tree, and hid it behind her back. She took me in front of the class, in front of my teacher and my class-mates. She whipped my behind and legs, repeating, "*Uzosubire!*" ("If you do that again…!") , which is not a fair translation because when said in Kirundi, it is a real threat! I started to cry. "Swallow your tears!" she said. It wasn't the physical pain that made me cry; it was the humiliation of being beaten in front of the whole class. From that day on, I was a good student and never messed around again.

On another occasion, Aunt Aurelia taught me values through some myths. Early on, I learned a certain myth that palm oil was forbidden to use, a kind of superstition that was believed by cattle owners. For instance, if I ate food with palm oil, I wasn't allowed to drink cow milk, or eat food with cow derived butter. However, sometimes I ate food with palm oil at my friend's house. Then later, I would forget and drink skim milk at home. When I would re-member what I had done, I would be so frightened of what would happen to our cows, but I kept silent from fear of repercussions from Grandpa. What if the myths were real and Grandpa's cows got hurt because of what I had done? Grownups told scary stories to children that if we did such things and ate the forbidden food, the cows' udders would fall off. Nothing of the sort happened, of course— at least nothing related to what we ate. So, quite often, I took on the habit of challenging this myth by eating what was forbidden, just to see what would happen.

I was once apprehended eating a fancy donut (called "*mandazi*" in Swahili) that I had been given by one of my friends at school. She was from the Swahili community where they made these donuts to sell. I saved it until I got home and was enjoying it when Aunt Aurelia saw me. "Where did you get that thing?" she quizzed me.

"I got it from my friend Amina at school," I said, my voice shaking in anticipation of her punishment.

"You naughty child," she said, grabbing my arm. "Don't you know you'll cause the cows' udders to fall? Do you want your grandfather to know about this? Why did you eat that kind of food?" Aunt Aurelia demanded.

"But—" I started.

"No buts! Give me that thing." She took the rest of my sweet donut and threw it far into the fields. And then she gave me the spanking of my life. When she was done, I ran and hid for a while. Thank God she didn't tell Grandpa. Even Aurelia was afraid of Grandfather's punishment for me. From then on, I decided that if I ever got a good sweet donut again, I would not show it to anyone. I would finish it at school and come home clean. Those donuts were the sweetest thing I had ever tasted. To this day, I still don't understand the reasons why there were such myths among cattle owners. What I do understand, however, is that drinking milk was a lot healthier for me as a little girl, than eating the *mandazi* full of saturated fats and loaded with sugar. Many such myths were used as a way of teaching good habits and other values to children.

Despite my being sheltered by my grandmother, she couldn't shield me from everything. She had to let the universe take care of me. That is exactly what happened the day she told me to go unleash our calf, which was grazing in the fields, and bring it home. I must have been ten or eleven years old when this happened. The sky had turned gray, and then dark, and seemed bloated and ready to explode. Everyone was in alert mode. I was going to bring the calf home when, all of a sudden, I fell into a ditch and lost consciousness for a few seconds. Then I woke up and smelled this weird smell on me. It was difficult to identify what kind of smell it was. I thought it smelled like something was burning, but I could not quite identify what—maybe burnt plastic. Minutes later, I felt a burn on my left forearm, and I realized I had been struck by lightning, but I was too weak to make any move. I started calling for help, calling my grandma, "Nyogokuru, Nyogo...Grandma..." but my voice was so weak, and in the middle of the thunder and lightning, my voice wasn't loud enough. I waited in the ditch to regain composure and, eventually some strength to call for help. Then I saw another bolt of lightning, followed by the sound of an angry thunder, and my whole body felt like a lifeless mass.

Barenga, my adopted aunt, was calling me and looking for me everywhere. I heard her call my name and I replied, but my voice was too weak for her to hear me. I also heard my grandmother calling my name, "Sakundaaaaa...!" I could hear how anxious her voice was, like she wasn't going to lose me to lightning strikes now when she had already saved my little life once. I remember making the Sign of the Cross in a very grown up way. It was like a knock on God's door, saying, "Please do not let me die and disappoint Grandma." At that very moment, I heard Barenga coming toward me, running frantically. She picked me up from the ditch and brought me in the house. She put me on the floor, and by then, my grandmother was crying nonstop.

The lightning must have really zapped me because my whole body was so weak that it felt like I had no bones, no muscles to put my little body together. My grandmother and Barenga, and whoever else was on the scene, started calling my name to revive me. Their calling went on and on for several minutes. I could hear them, but I felt both present and absent, as if floating in a world I didn't understand, but I wasn't in pain. After a couple of minutes of their calling my name and reviving me, I tried to be strong for

Grandma. I wanted to speak, but words wouldn't come out. Then I tried to reassure her with non-verbal communication signs to tell her I was alive but just weak. I wanted to tell Grandma I wasn't dying; that I only needed to sleep, to get a little rest. But Grandma was too anguished to pay attention to what I was trying to communicate. I could tell she had already lost hope that I could survive the lightning strike. I just stayed on that floor, waiting to regain my strength, as I watched her cry endlessly. I don't know what I did after a moment, but it was then that they stopped calling my name. All of a sudden, they relaxed and were relieved that I had made it. I later told my grandmother that it was kind of nice to have a sneak peek to see who would cry if I died. (Naughty child even at my deathbed, huh!)

Whew! There I was, revived and alive, my blood flowing at its normal rate again. I started telling them what had happened, and how God had saved me because I had made the Sign of the Cross. My grandmother started performing some of her traditional medicine on the burn that the lightning had left on my forearm; the very same left arm that had been burnt when I was a crawling baby. It was the only part affected by this tropical storm.

After two weeks, the burn started developing an infection. I went to the dispensary near my school, even though it was believed that only traditional medicine, not modern medicine, should be used in the case of a lightning burn. I went despite my grandmother's pleas never to use modern medicine. I guess I had an attitude at that age, so I would not listen to her. The nurse put some cream on the burn, and it healed the very same week. The clinic staff congratulated me on beating the lightning and staying alive. I still have the scar on my left forearm. Each time I am distraught, I look at it and remember how God again saved me from dying at such a young age.

CHAPTER 1 EVOLVING QUESTIONS FOR REFLECTION

1. What childhood memories do you have that shaped your growing up?

_____

_____

_____

_____

_____

2. What have you learned from those memories that helped/or can help you become a stronger you?

_____

_____

_____

_____

_____

3. Who are the people involved in those memories and how influential were they in your evolvement?

_____

_____

_____

_____

_____

Chapter 2

REFLECTING ON MY ORIGINS

Today you are you! That is truer than true!
There is no one alive who is you-er than you!
— Dr. Seuss

My name is Seconde Nimenya. My last name roughly translates as "only God knows." In my native country of Burundi, many last names include God, especially for Christians. Others, however, reveal how a family copes with life's circumstances. You may hear names with a victory meaning, or names with a victim meaning. My first name, Seconde, however, takes its roots from the Latin name of Secunda. My mother was a fluent reader of the Latin Bible that was introduced in the early nineteenth century into Africa by the Roman Catholic Church. Although my family calls me Sekunda (they dropped the C for the K), in high school, students called me Seconde, and I ended up keeping it that way to make it sound French. Whenever an English speaker asks me my name and I say, "Seconde," pronounced *"Segonde,"* they usually hear Sigourney. Maybe I should change it to Sigourney! I've decided that if I ever change my name, it would be fully American with a middle name to boot.

People also like to ask me the meaning of my first name. I usually tell them the meaning in French, which is "second," as in a numerical order. Then they ask whether I am the second-born. Well, I am the fifth out of seven children. As if my name didn't sound mysterious enough, I also have to contend with a mysterious English accent. Each time I talk with an American, I get the compliment that I've come to take for granted. "You have a beautiful accent!"

"Thank you!" I respond. But as much as I enjoy the compliment, I also dread the usual follow up question, "Where are you from?" Then the insecure me thinks, "Gosh, why can't I melt into the crowd and look and speak like Americans instead of always sticking out as an outsider?" I've tried to tell people, "I am Canadian." But for a second, they will ponder my answer, give me a once over, and not be easily fooled. So, next comes, "But where do you come from originally?" with a fat emphasis on originally. At this point, I can't continue to fake my origins. I didn't actually know I had been playing this game until my two teenage daughters once sat me down, and said "Mom, we've noticed that each time someone asks you where you come from, you lie!" Gee, thanks girls. I might have wanted to fake my origins for reasons that are not obvious to most Americans. Coming from a country that's known for being war-torn and makes the list of poorest in the world every year, I thought that maybe if I just forgot about it, and focused on being my adoptive country's full citizen, it would lessen the pain I feel about my native country.

Since I now live here in the beautiful United States of America, I have started considering that people's questions might be well intended. They want to get to know me and my origins, and maybe they want to connect with me. Most want to learn something new by asking questions about places they've never been. When I let my guard down and say, "I come from Burundi," we get to another level of questions, and this time, I feel compelled to explain where my homeland is located. Depending on people's interest, I throw in a little bit of history and even politics. Sometimes, people ask me, "Is Burundi an exotic island?" No, it's not an island, but it has the same kind of beauty as any exotic place.

I don't think many folks here in America know that Burundi is even a country. Sometimes even I have a hard time finding it on the African map. It looks like a dot, a little drop in a big ocean, as Burundian singers so eloquently used to put it. When she was in middle school, my middle child Elva told me that she had been taught about Africa in social studies. "That's a good thing, sweetie!" I said proudly. But then Elva said, "It's so boring Mom; we can't wait for this subject to be over!" I bet it was boring. It bored me too when I was in high school learning about those weird names of old African tribes. What teenager in his or her right mind needs to learn about the *Mossi* Empire or the *Mandingue* tribe? We were also asked to memorize country capitals in a song (and that's how I still remember a couple of them), presidents around the world, and all Burundi's government ministers and other high ranking politicians' names. At every *coup d'état* or reelection, they changed them, and we had to start all over again.

It was only after I was grown that I realized what a wealth of knowledge I had about the world in general. So, I told Elva that she should strive to learn about Africa because it's the second largest continent both in area and population, but its history is the least known. My husband, Claver, who is also from Burundi, told me a story about when he first arrived in Canada. He rode a bus from Mirabel airport in Montreal to Sherbrooke, where he was going to study for his master's degree. On the bus, he met a passenger, and they started chatting.

"Where are you from?" the passenger asked him.

"I come from Burundi," Claver told him.

"Where is that?" the passenger asked.

"It's in Africa," my husband informed the man.

"Do you guys have houses in Africa?" the passenger asked, really wanting to know.

"Oh, no! We live in trees. As a matter of fact, your ambassador lives in the biggest tree because he has an important job," Claver answered. The passenger didn't reply; and I'm not sure he understood that Claver was only joking.

Because of such situations, I was excited when my daughter said they were learning about Africa in social studies; it's the only way to shed some light on the continent, one country at a time.

Burundi is a small landlocked country located in East-Central Africa. It is bordered by Rwanda on the north, the Democratic Republic of Congo on the west, and Tanzania on the east. It covers only 10,745 square miles with a population of 10,557,259 according to a 2012 estimate. Burundi's capital and largest city is Bujumbura. Kirundi and French are its two official languages. Swahili is spoken mainly in Bujumbura and other commercial centers, and it is often a language of communication between Burundians and their eastern counterparts, such as Tanzanians and Kenyans. The weather is temperate; only Bujumbura, located alongside Lake Tanganyika, is hot and humid. When it comes to the climate, Burundi is a paradise on Earth. Its evergreen forests, mild temperatures, lakes, exotic birds, and endless pastures offer an enjoyable panorama that has long been the envy of Westerners.

Many foreigners adore Burundi. I met an American man on the plane when I went to visit my family in 2006 who was working for the United Nations on a reconstruction mission in Burundi.

He was in his late fifties, tanned by the zenith sun, and had a thick goatee.

"Do you like it in Burundi?" I asked him.

"I have fallen in love with Burundi. Out of all the underdeveloped countries I have been assigned to, Burundi is by far the best place," he said, adding that the people were cheerful despite their problems and poverty. He found the weather to be clement, and he said to be there was an indulgence for a Westerner used to rough winters.

"That's true," I nodded. I used to think there was no better place to live on Earth before I left Burundi in 1992. When I was a little girl living with my grandparents, I recall running outside, basking in the sun, especially in the summer months. I would pirouette to let the wind lift up my skirts to show off my underwear when I started wearing them in first grade.

After we landed at the Bujumbura airport, I saw my American acquaintance kissing a girl who had come to welcome him. On my way back to America, we met again, and while waiting for our connecting flight at the Addis Ababa International Airport in Ethiopia, I saw him hugging and then kissing this cute Ethiopian girl. No wonder he liked it out there; he had wonderful UN benefits!

My hometown is in southern Burundi, in the province of Makamba. My parents have always lived in Vugizo, a small town in the southwest of the province. Vugizo's nickname is "la Suisse" because of its landscape similarities with Switzerland. It is a high rough plateau on the side of a group of mountains, Mount Inanzegwe being the highest in the region at 7064 feet elevation. The climate in Vugizo is also a little chillier than in the lower landscapes of the rest of Makamba. It rains a lot during rainy season (December to April) and is often foggier in Vugizo than in the rest of the province. It is windy and dry during the dry season (July to

August). The months of September to November are called small wet season because it rains, but not as heavily as the rainy season months. Also, the months of May to June are called the small dry season, as it is dry but not as dry as the months of July and August.

My hometown's main challenge is the lack of good roads due to its geographic landscape. Because of the rough mountains and hillsides surrounding the town, it has always been difficult for the government to build decent roads. There is only one road that connects to Vugizo, no matter what direction you are coming from. Students from other parts of the country used to tease Vugizo natives about there being only one road, "the road to Vugizo." You have to take other major roads that go to the city of Makamba's city center, and then take the connecting road from there to Vugizo—a bumpy ride to say the least. So much for being like Switzerland! But during my university years in the capital, I was always excited whenever I reached that bumpy road when I went to visit my parents. The landscape—mountains and endless hills—is breathtaking. It felt like home to me, and I wouldn't have traded it for any other place.

But the last time I visited my parents, I complained a lot about the road's conditions. After almost fifteen years of enjoying the comfort of North American roads and highways, I felt discomfort on the bumpy road. Those who were traveling with me kept apologizing for the road's conditions, as if it were their fault. They also asked me to compare the road to the ones in America. Well, where should I have begun? Should I have described all the interstates? How about the beautiful bridges? But I knew what their questions implied. How could this tiny country, their beloved Burundi, not have decent roads, when big countries like Canada or the United States have all those highways and bridges? I simply told them that it was impossible to compare Burundi to the U.S. or Canada because of their differences in economic development.

Fortunately, the bumpy road is only an hour's drive, and before I knew it, we were at my parents' home. My son Darrel, who was with me on that trip, was so amazed by what he saw that he still talks about it with awe to his sisters. For him, seeing cows, chickens, and goats, up close and personal, was the most amazing experience he had ever had. And I was happy that, at six years old, he got to experience the difference between his life in North America and life in Burundi. He had a blast and appreciated everything he saw. Darrel amazed me with how he adapted to the people he was seeing for the first time. I especially loved seeing him bond with my mother, even though he didn't speak Kirundi, and she was unable to speak English or French. But the two communicated their love through a non-verbal language, and wherever my mother went, Darrel followed. To me, this was a testimony that love truly doesn't speak any language because love is the language.

My son took every opportunity to run outside and play without the restrictions I put on him when we are in America. He felt free to talk to strangers for no particular reason. He actually thought anyone who was black was related to us. In my hometown, my son and I were special guests. All my neighbors came to welcome us, and they even danced for us till the wee hours. I was amused by one of my neighbors, a man in his late seventies, who knows a thing or two about riches. He asked me, "So, tell me my child, I hear America is beautiful. Is it true that it's sparkling, and has marble everywhere you go?"

"Oh yes, marble is everywhere!" I said. I couldn't bring myself to spoil his enthusiasm and knowledge about America. In another instance, Darrel was the one particularly impressed. On our way back to Bujumbura from my parents' house, we met school kids in their khaki uniforms, going back home. It was a wet day. It had been raining for three steady consecutive days. This was February, the middle of the rainy season. Our pickup truck got stuck in the mud, and couldn't move. Some of the kids were my son's age, if not younger. But, they climbed the pickup truck as it kept sliding in the mud, and moving in spirals. One of the kids yelled at our driver, "You don't know how to drive? Pass me the wheel!" Despite their apparent poverty, these kids seemed happy, loud, and free to be just kids. Most of them do not get to see cars up-close often, which is why they came to our spiraling pickup to experience the spectacle when they saw it moving slowly. The driver had to chase them away to get them off the vehicle, and they ran giggling.

Those kids reminded me of my elementary school years, those early times when I would walk two hours to go to school with my big sister Claire yelling at me because I wasn't fast enough. Some days, I just couldn't take it anymore, so I would drop on the ground crying. Claire would grab my hand, and literally drag me behind her. Back in those days, schools were only found at major commercial centers, where Arabic merchants had established Swahili communities before the colonization by Germany and then Belgium in the early twentieth century. The colonizers had then built schools following in the steps of those commercial centers. When I was in elementary school, it was very common in many parts of the country only to have one primary school within twenty to thirty miles, and we had no school buses. Nowadays, they have elementary schools located within as little as five miles walking distance, something I never thought would be possible in my lifetime.

CHAPTER 2 EVOLVING QUESTIONS FOR REFLECTION

1. Take a moment to reflect on your roots; do you know your origins?

_____

_____

_____

_____

_____

2. Was there a time when you had mixed or conflicting feelings about your origins?

_____

_____

_____

_____

3. If so, what did those feelings and emotions ignite in you?

_____

_____

_____

_____

Chapter 3
UNDERSTANDING THE HISTORICAL CONTEXT

Those who do not remember the past are condemned to repeat it.
— George Santayana

Given its geographical location, Burundi never experienced slavery. Only the West African countries went through the slave trade period. Before the Germans came to colonize, Burundi was already organized with an administration. It was a kingdom with kings, chiefs, and sub-chiefs. The kingdom was divided into territories and chief-towns, led by chiefs. Although in Burundian history, the royal families were identified as the upper class, set apart from the masses, they belonged to the Tutsi ethnic group. Tutsis, Hutus, and Batwa constituted the ethnic groups that lived in Burundi at least five hundred years ago. The Batwa were the minority (1 percent of the population) choosing to live apart, and not mingle with the rest of the population. The Batwa have always been a semi-nomadic people, and they claim to have inhabited the Great Lakes region of central Africa as the first population, living by hunting wild animals. They never had any significant political role in Burundi, and they were often ignored in the political power balance. When I was a child living with my grandparents, Batwas used to come to our home to sell us pottery, an art in which they were very good. They walked around semi-naked and lived in locations where outside influence didn't reach them.

Therefore, the two main ethnic groups in Burundi were the Tutsis and the Hutus. The people paid tribute to the mwami or king who owned all the land. The throne passed from father to son within the different royal clans. The main wars were against the neighboring territories, to extend Burundi's geographical boundaries. In the late 1790s, under King Ntare Rugamba, Burundi's size almost doubled.

In the 1890s, Burundi became a German colony. In 1919, after Germany was defeated in World War I, the Versailles Treaty redistributed all German colonies. By the early twentieth century after Germany's defeat, Belgium, one of the Allies that had won the war, was given both Burundi and Rwanda to govern. The notion of race and tribalism wasn't on the minds of Burundians at that time. Tutsis and Hutus didn't hate each other on the basis of their ethnic belonging; people never used machetes or guns to kill each other. As a matter of fact, they lived together in harmony. Each ethnic group had chosen different occupations to earn its livelihood. Each accepted its living conditions and produced what it needed on the tenured land. Tutsis were usually cattle owners while Hutus were farmers. This division of labor formed a perfectly balanced traditional economy in Burundi. The exchanges were a part of the economic system that allowed for obtaining what one didn't produce or make. Unfortunately, that division of work came to have a negative connotation during colonial times.

Race and class surfaced because the European powers were used to having a class system. Therefore, to govern Burundi, they introduced the same division in classes. The colonizers got one ethnic group to look down on the other, and divided them to assert their power. They purposely weakened the relationship between the Tutsis and Hutus, using their motto of "divide and reign." Evidently, the well-established Burundian aristocracy was seen by Belgians as a superior class since it had governed Burundi for centuries. The division in economical activities became the Belgians' first criteria for class division. Hutus, who had labored on the land for centuries, were now seen by Europeans as the "masses" or lower class. Tutsis, who loved to tend to their cattle so much, were said to have migrated from northern East Africa. Some history books about the two ethnic groups' origins contain theories implying that Tutsis were an arrogant population that descended from the Nilotics (descendants of ethnic groups from southern Ethiopia, Uganda, Kenya, and northern Tanzania) and imposed themselves and their cattle on the central populations of Hutus living off agriculture.

I suppose the migration literature is true; Tutsis had to come from somewhere like everyone else. I used to argue about it when I was in my medieval history class at the University of Burundi whenever our professor would teach us about feudal life. He would say that what the literature suggested regarding the migrations and differences in lifestyle between the Tutsis and Hutus wasn't necessarily true. But I would raise my hand and with a timid high pitched voice and say, "What's wrong with the Tutsis descending from the Nilotics? Both Hutus and Tutsis migrated, and it doesn't provide reason to kill either group." I never understood why these migration theories stirred so much hatred among Burundians. The professor would look at me, smile, and dismiss my naïveté. "What I don't agree with is the 'arrogant and imposing' part," I would continue, realizing that I was aggravating our professor's patience. That year, at the University of Burundi, there were rumors that some Hutu students had machetes in their dorms—rumors no one could prove true or false. Therefore, our professor was trying to avoid adding any more fuel to the fire at the university since students of both ethnic groups were very sensitive to this kind of information about ethnical belonging.

These books also discuss the physical descriptions of each ethnicity, and reading them, again, you have to keep an open mind, and not automatically accept everything you're told. Tutsis were described as being sharp-nosed, tall, and having clear skin. They were also assumed to be smarter, closer to whites, and therefore, worth educating and preparing for political positions. This made the Hutus feel inferior, not beautiful, and unworthy. Therefore, all these psychological messages got into many people's heads and provoked hatred. Most of the academic books written on Burundi to discuss these clichés and stereotype issues have been written by Europeans who really didn't know Burundians. Many have only succeeded into confusing racialist theories and class systems with migration hypotheses.

For one thing, if I were to believe in these physical descriptions, my height (5'3"—okay, 5'4" with high heels!) or my big brother Emmanuel's skin color (ebony) would be questioned. When Emmanuel was in elementary school, he was discriminated against by his fourth grade teacher. His teacher once saw my dad at my brother's school and asked him, "Are you Emmanuel's real father?" Because my father is clear-skinned and has a sharp nose, the Tutsi teacher didn't believe Emmanuel could be my dad's son. The teacher thought Emmanuel must be a Hutu just because of his flat nose and darker skin. That was in the aftermath of the killings of 1972, and my brother was being discriminated against by those who should have protected him. If he were in a Hutu teacher's classroom, he wouldn't have been spared either; he would have been discriminated against, because he was Tutsi since Hutus knew how to identify someone beyond his looks.

Given the advantages some Tutsis were reaping from the Belgian administration, some Hutus wanted to "become Tutsis" and were allowed to do so by what was called "*Kwihutura*," literally meaning losing the Hutu characteristics or identity, to become Tutsi. Hutus could achieve this by changing their social and economic standing, such as owning more cattle, and farming lesser lands, and for Hutu men, marrying Tutsi women. They would choose to socialize more with Tutsis than Hutus and would want to be seen in Tutsi company. Although the phenomenon of Kwihutura was very minimal, you can see how those who bought into this philosophy were denying their self-worth, to belong to the more privileged class. Belgians made sure opportunities were denied to most Hutus, and even many Tutsis who weren't affiliated with the kings, either by marriage or other affiliation didn't appear to benefit. Thus, the gap between the two ethnicities was widened, and the creation of classes among the Tutsis started to appear.

Even though Hutus could become Tutsis by sheer social and economical transformation, they couldn't escape the physical descriptions that Belgians attached to all Burundians. The large nose, height of their foreheads, their heights, and other physical traits were how each ethnicity was determined. However, many exceptions fell into one or the other of the categories, especially interethnical offspring. You can imagine the frustration of Hutus who had to go through this transformation to become Tutsis, only still be Hutu in the end. This situation only festered in anger and other negative emotions among the Hutus, who eventually exploded after the Belgians left.

Although Belgians introduced the school system as we know it today in Burundi, they didn't leave any other remarkable legacies. The little development they brought to the country consisted of road construction and was done by the Burundian people, the so called "HAV" in French for *Homme Adulte et Valide* (healthy and strong adult male). These were adolescent and older males who were strongly built and healthy, forced to work in road construction. Colonizers also forced Burundians to cultivate crops for European consumption, especially coffee and tea; to be their carriers and laborers, and to pay hefty taxes. If Burundians broke the Belgians' rules, they were not just punished; they were publicly shamed and severely beaten. My grandfather used to tell me that in his time during the colonization, men were beaten up, forced to drop their pants, and whipped (with a big whip called *Ikimoko*) on their behinds until they bled. Most times, the chiefs were forced to perform the whipping on their fellow Burundians, which made the beatings even more humiliating.

When Belgians realized what they had done to Burundi's political and socio-economic balance, they tried to reverse it by promoting Hutus and helping them avoid any Tutsi dominance. Such supports resulted in helping the Christian Democratic Party (Parti Democrate Chrétien) that was pro-Belgian to oppose the progressive nationalist movement founded by Prince Louis Rwagasore, King Mwambutsa IV's oldest son. Prince Louis Rwagasore had a vision for a post-colonial Burundi. He was Burundi's visionary and promoted nationalism and the end of colonization. He became Burundi's prime minister after winning the first elections in 1961, in which his party Union for National Progress won 80 percent of the votes. Prince Rwagasore wasn't liked by Belgians, evidently because he was promoting Burundi's independence. He was assassinated by a Greek mercenary named Georges Kageorgis in the middle of his dinner at the Hotel Tanganyika in Bujumbura, on October 13, 1961. Prince Rwagasore was said to be an all inclusive-man, who was trying to bridge the monarchy, the population, and the ethnicities. Himself a Tutsi, he was married to a Hutu woman.

However, his dreams for the country were terminated after his life was ended at the young age of twenty-nine.

The stereotypes used to divide the two ethnic groups certainly achieved the colonizers' goal, because to this day, they still occupy Burundians' collective conscience. I truly believe that we Burundians are not interested in knowing whether we came from people who were white, black, red, or any color in between. We don't care whether we're tall, short or average, or whether we have sharp or flat noses. We're interested in having our humanity respected. No one's life deserves to be taken away because he or she has clear skin, dark skin, or anything in the middle. As it has been stated by many who have written about the different ethnical wars, people who kill or want to kill in the name of ethnic belonging— or for any other reason for that matter— act out of evil because they allow themselves to be fed with evil information. We don't need another ethnology research study to understand the need to respect life.

My maternal grandfather used to sing to me the song Burundians sang when the Belgians left: "Ababirigi baragiye sangwa Burundi we" which means: "Belgians have left, glory to Burundi!" It was a cheering song that celebrated the colonization's end in 1962.

CHAPTER 3 EVOLVING QUESTIONS FOR REFLECTION

1. Looking back on your own country's historical past, do you see any pattern you may have inherited as part of your personal history?

_____

_____

_____

_____

_____

2. For instance, did you attend a segregated school, which affected how you view the world, yourself, or others, or did you witness others being discriminated against while you were among the privileged category? Take a moment and reflect on that.

_____

_____

_____

_____

_____

3. If you had the opportunity to rebuild the history of your country, what would you change?

_____

_____

_____

_____

_____

Chapter 4

HAVING AN INNOCENT MIND

An eye for an eye only ends up making the whole world blind.
—Mahatma Gandhi

When I started first grade, it was Aunt Aurelia who took me to school, first for registration and then on the first day of school. That summer before school started, she had been preparing me to begin school. Aunt Aurelia wasn't literate, but she knew math. She taught me how to count up to twenty, which was all I needed to qualify for first grade admission. She showed me how to count to twenty using my fingers and toes. One day, she sat me down, demonstrated for me, and then said, "Now it's your turn, add up all your fingers."

So, I did and started counting. "One, two, three, four, five, six, seven, eight, nine, ten!" I said proudly.

"Now, add your fingers to your toes, and in the same way, count how many you have together," Aunt Aurelia told me. I did as she asked, and magically, I could count up to twenty, using my fingers and my toes. It was the first time I realized I had ten fingers and ten toes. Quite a discovery! It was my mother's brother, Uncle

Apollinaire, who paid for my enrollment in the elementary school despite my grandmother's pleas. Grandma would have preferred me to attend the catechism classes and graduate with a set of sacraments. Catechism education was shorter than elementary school and limited to only basic cursive writing and reading. My grandmother found regular school tortuous, and she loved me too much to put me through that trauma. At that time, girls were not expected to attend school. Finding a husband and having numerous kids, was their ultimate achievement.

Before I became school material, I had lived in a little cocoon world, protected and loved by my grandmother. All that changed in April of 1972. It was a day my big sister Claire and I should have stayed home. Instead, we woke up early as usual, packed our lunches, and walked the usual two-and-a-half hours to school. Claire was in sixth grade and I was in first grade at l' École Primaire des Filles de Makamba, a girls only primary school.

Around mid-morning that day, parents began dropping by the school one by one, entering the principal's office. Then, I saw a parent come to our classroom, and my teacher went to talk to the parent outside the classroom, carefully closing the door behind her. Then the teacher came into the classroom, called one student's name, and told her to join her parent, who was waiting outside. The girl gathered her belongings and left. Next thing I knew, another parent came in, talked to the teacher, and once more, the same scenario occurred. Young as I was, I jumped to one conclusion: "Oooooh, the little girl is in trrrrouble!" I thought to myself. Yet, the way my little classmates gathered their belongings made me feel uneasy. We always left our notebooks and chalkboards in our desks at school. Therefore, when I saw them leaving one by one with all their belongings, I thought they must have been bad pupils. Little did I know that their early dismissal was due to insider information. Their parents had heard there was an ongoing attack in the country.

Shortly after, the principal called all the teachers and informed them that the rest of the kids had to be released immediately. That is when we learned that some Hutu militias, the *mayi mulele* as they called themselves, had started killing Tutsis in some areas of the country including my parents' hometown of Vugizo. Men and boys were the main targets. My father was away in East Africa, so it was left to my mother to protect her children.

Although the word went out that Hutus were attacking Tutsis, it didn't register in my mind. I didn't feel any particular fear. I didn't know what ethnic group I belonged to; it was something my grandparents never talked about. They had adopted a mother with a mental illness and her daughter Barenga, who were of Hutu ethnicity. I suspect my grandparents didn't talk about ethnic matters because they were an all inclusive family and they never mentioned the words Hutu or Tutsi. They valued every human being for who that person was, and not what he or she might be. These were the values I was brought up with. Most of my childhood friends and the majority of my classmates were of the Hutu ethnic group. Therefore, I connected with kids my age, regardless of their ethnicities.

How could a kid my age understand that people were killing each other in the name of ethnic belonging? Sometimes when I think of that day, I realize something about those parents who came early to pick up their kids. They were rich parents, meaning the province's elite, who lived near the city center, not far from our school. They were informed of what was going on in the country because they were members of the province's administrative branch. The other group was of Hutu ethnicity, they knew about the civil war because they had been involved in its preparation. But the majority of Tutsi students, and even some Hutus who lived far away from the school, didn't get picked up; nor did our parents get the memo. We didn't know what was going on until the school decided to release the rest of us all at once. We were told that there was a war going on between the government army and the militia mobs, the so called *mayi mulele*. We had to go straight home immediately. My sister Claire came to my classroom, grabbed my arm as if I had caused the trouble, and instructed me that we had to go home right away. Many of the kids hadn't been picked up earlier, and since we were released all at the same time, we seemed to fill the roads, running to get home.

I wasn't scared. Because of my childhood innocence, I didn't think of what those bad guys would do to us if they got hold of us. Who would want to kill a little girl? In addition, I relied on my big sister to protect me should anybody want to mess with me; Claire always defended me. My big sister seemed troubled because she understood what was going on. Older kids explained what was going to happen from bits of information they had. In my brain, it all sounded like waves from an unfriendly river, and I could not focus or make any sense out of it. I had heard someone mention that the militias were recognized by their chanting "*mayi mulele*," so I started a song in my head with the words "*mayi mulele*." That little song got me in trouble when I started singing it first in whispers, and then out loud. My sister Claire heard me singing and she yelled at me, hoping I would stop, but the song was so stuck in my head. I didn't know those were bad words or even dangerous words because they identified the bad guys. I kept singing in whispers, but my sister took on the assignment of making sure I stopped singing those ugly words. She started hitting me each time I sang, and that's what it took to get me to stop.

When we arrived home that day, my grandparents had already learned about the war, and my grandmother was afraid of what might happen to us. She looked at my sister and me with frightened eyes, not knowing how she would protect us from the killings. A Hutu neighbor had informed my grandparents of what he knew about these killings, but he reassured my grandfather that he would never hurt us. We were practically the only Tutsi family in our village. So, if the Hutus in our village wanted, they could have killed us overnight, and no questions would have been asked. But instead, they continued to be the good neighbors they had always been. They viewed my grandfather as someone they could count on when they were in a difficulty, especially with regards to land conflicts. He was their *Umushingantahe* (sage man), – an honorable mentor whom they called upon to help them settle their problems. My grandmother also helped their families whenever they fell short on food. She would go to the family farm, harvest as much as she could, and split it into shares. She would then appoint me to bring the food to many of our Hutu neighbors. If we ran out of salt before the next market day, I was sent to borrow salt for the night at our Hutu neighbor. For Burundians at that time, borrowing salt was a strong sign of trust. Because salt was a rare commodity, people didn't waste it by giving it if they didn't trust you would do the same when they had a shortage of it. In addition, the lack of salt showed vulnerability that only your trusted friends could know about.

We had a very good relationship with our Hutu neighbors and were grateful that they didn't turn against us as it happened in other parts of the country. Many Tutsi families had already been killed elsewhere in the country, and it was just a matter of time before the war would reach us. Many Tutsis had fled their villages in anticipation of what was going to happen. As soon as the radio started broadcasting news, my grandfather glued his ear to the transistor. Grandpa had long since established sole custody of the radio. No one was allowed to talk, let alone kids being allowed to play or scream, during the broadcasting. We learned from the news that some Hutus had taken machetes and killed their Tutsi neighbors. It was reported that this war was an act of ethnic cleansing to bring equilibrium in the government and army. It was alleged that the Tutsis were the majority in the government and army, but those who perished were villagers who barely knew anything about politics. Again, all this sunk in my head once I was old enough to understand during the subsequent wars. But at that time, I didn't feel any danger. I relied on the adults to protect me.

That night, we didn't sleep in the house. Everybody was hiding and so did we. Hiding places consisted of nearby bushes where we slept under the moon. Grandpa was concerned about his cows, but we left them home, where surprisingly, they stayed still, as if they too sensed the danger. Aunt Katarina, one of my mom's sisters who lived across the valley from us, joined us with her five children. I was very excited to see my cousins, but kids were quickly told not to move a finger. We were told to be on our best behaviors or else. However, my grandmother's asthma attacked her with a vengeance; she coughed all night long. That was the only time I was scared that the bad guys might locate us and kill my grandma. Other than that, I felt as if we were summer camping, only it was April. April in Burundi is a heavy rainy month. Usually rain in April is accompanied by thunderstorms, heavy winds, and flooding. Indeed, we had rain that night —a lightning thunderstorm— and we were forced to retreat to the house. So we got to a point where we would rather be killed by Hutus than be struck by lightning.

The Hutus purposely had started the war in April because of the heavy rain, so Tutsis would be forced to stay in their homes. My parents' hometown was severely affected by the war, and we were very worried that my mom and my siblings might have been killed. We continued to live normally during the day, adults attending to their normal labors, and we resumed hiding at night, as if death only comes in the night. Anyone who has been to Africa knows how dark African nights are, especially in the countryside where there is no electricity.

By the end of July 1972, Makamba, my grandparents' hometown, was clear of danger. It wasn't as affected by the war as other regions in the south, mostly because the majority of the population was of Hutus. On the other hand, reports said that in the south of Burundi, one of the most affected towns was Vugizo, my parents' hometown. My mother ventured out, took my five siblings, and came to Makamba to take refuge at her parents' house. We were so happy to see them alive. They had escaped by hiding in the mountains during the nights, especially Mount Inanzegwe, where many lives had been saved. During the day, they went home to continue their regular chores, and at night, they retreated to the bushes and mountains. They told us how my three brothers would have been killed if my mom had not disguised them in girls' clothes. She told us about one particular close call.

That day, my mother and siblings had come home for the regular day work and to make some food to take to their hiding place. Mom had just finished dressing my youngest baby brother in a cute little dress she had borrowed from one of my little cousins. She had just put him on her back when a member of the militia (who was also one of my parents' neighbors) appeared out of nowhere and summoned my mother to show the sex of the baby. He said, "That baby must be a boy; let him off your back and let me check."

"No, she's a girl, don't you know?" Mom said.

"I am sure that baby's a boy. Now let him off your back or I'll kill you both," the militia man threatened.

"You better kill me first before you touch my baby," my mother challenged. They argued back and forth for a while, and miraculously, the militia man gave in and continued his man-hunting elsewhere. By then, my two older brothers had slipped into a long hole they used to ripen bananas and covered themselves with banana leaves; they could barely breathe. The killer walked right by the hole and didn't see them, and that's how they escaped.

This man-hunt was believed to be the Hutus' strategy to eliminate the Tutsi from procreating. They thought that by killing all Tutsi men and boys (including babies) and marrying the Tutsi women, they would enable only Hutus offspring, and the country would be all Hutu in subsequent generations. My mother was already assigned to some Hutu neighbor to take her once the war would end. My paternal aunt Domitile's husband was hunted down and nearly killed by his Hutu neighbors, who were competing to marry my aunt. They said she was the most beautiful woman in the village, and they almost killed each other arguing over who would marry her. Aunt Domitile was my favorite auntie when I was growing up. Sleepovers at her house were always a pleasure; she treated me as a special guest whenever I visited her. Thankfully, her husband escaped those Hutu killings. Many of my classmates lost their loved ones. My Hutu best friend Seraphine's two brothers were killed while away at boarding high school. Many Tutsis and Hutus alike were killed in the name of ethical belonging, and similar deaths continue to haunt Burundi to this day.

CHAPTER 4 EVOLVING QUESTIONS FOR REFLECTION

1. Were you or your parents ever affected by any war any time in your life?

_____

_____

_____

_____

_____

2. If so, which one, and how did you/your parents cope?

_____

_____

_____

_____

_____

3. What did you learn about yourself and humanity in general from those events?

_____

_____

_____

_____

_____

Chapter 5

SHIFTING INTO NEW ROLES

In the end, it's not the years in your life that count.
It's the life in your years.
— Abraham Lincoln

When my sister Claire left school after she failed sixth grade many times, she went to live with my parents for good. I was the only one left living with my maternal grandparents, whose health was deteriorating by the day. At school, for the first time, I had to look out for myself since my big sister was no longer there to protect me. Although I had occasional visits from my cousins who lived nearby, I felt mostly like an only child, so I longed to live with my family and all my siblings. I missed my sister Claire, even her bossing me around. One good thing about having Claire at the same school was that she protected me against bullies both real and imagined. As soon as she left the school, all of a sudden, bullies were everywhere. Mediatrice, Seraphine, and I were constantly harassed by older boys from the school's neighborhood. One group of boys followed us every day after school. We did our best to run from them, but they were faster, and sometimes threw rocks at us, which to me was scarier than running after us because we could have been injured. We were afraid to tell our parents about these bullies because they were boys; our parents would have assumed that we were fooling with them, and we would have been the ones in trouble. Girls were always the ones in trouble because we were taught to avoid boys, and especially, not to "provoke" them. So, if a girl fell prey to a boy, it was her own fault, and parents usually didn't take her side. Therefore, we knew better than to tell our parents about our boy trouble.

We thought about reporting the boys at their school, but we learned that they were school dropouts. We knew where they lived, but we were too afraid to tell on them to their parents. So this bullying went on for several months until one day I told my friends that we needed to stand up for ourselves. My friends thought I was crazy since I was the tiniest of us, but I insisted that we had to do something if we wanted to stay in school and alive. At that point, I knew I needed to stay in school and achieve some education. I didn't want Uncle Apollinaire's money to be wasted, so I was committed to pursuing education after the time I had gotten in trouble for skipping school in third grade.

One day, my friends and I were leaving the school and going home. We were anxious as usual about meeting the bullies. Some days, they hid around the block in the back of the school, making us think they weren't coming that day, so we would start celebrating. But then we would see them resurface out of nowhere to frighten us. They didn't hurt us so much as make us exhausted from running away from them. That day, after I had told my friends that we would stand up to the bullies and they had agreed, the bullies came, and started following us. As soon as we saw them, my friends started running. So much for standing up for ourselves! But I refused to run. I stood there and faced the bullies. When one of the boys started touching my hand, I pushed him. Then I said, "I am going to report you to my parents, who will tell my school, and the school will tell your parents, and you guys are going to get in big trouble." How I thought about that I don't really know. All I know is that I felt like David facing Goliath. After a couple of minutes of this confrontation, they gave up and ran, calling me names, which didn't bother me. My friends had been watching the confrontation from a distance; they looked like frightened chickens, but they were amazed by how I had managed not to get killed. They couldn't believe that tiny Seconde had saved them from bullies. That day, we ran home, happy and free. The bullies disappeared altogether, and we never saw them again.

Now that I was older, I could make the trip to school in about an hour, mostly running, so I had to leave early every morning. I remember what my grandmother used to say, "If it weren't for your Uncle Apollinaire, you'd be attending catechism school and be nearly done." She insisted that the entire schooling trauma was her son's fault. I can still see her saddened face as she woke me up every morning, wheezing from her chronic asthma, and talking between coughs, calling me Sakunda. Catechism education was only two days a week, not every day like the regular school. All I needed was first communion and confirmation, and then no more studying, only attending Sunday Mass with Aunt Aurelia. Grandma wasn't Catholic, but she believed in something. She mostly worshipped God through the elements of Nature and the greater universe. But she knew that for my generation, the time had come to be religious and belong to the new beliefs brought by Europeans. To my grandmother, even though I didn't need school, she knew I needed to have sacraments. After all, I had been baptized when I was eleven days old.

Although Grandma didn't go to church or practice religion in the formal way Catholics did, she worshipped a Higher Power that she actually called God (*Imana* in Kirundi). She always ordered that we keep clean drinking water for when God would visit us overnight because He might be thirsty. Now that I look back at how she practiced her spirituality, I realize Grandma used the same practices that today are forward thinking for spiritual living. She used symbols, amulets, even meditations. As a child who was raised in the full bloom of a Catholic school, I silently criticized Grandma's ancient practices. To me, they were not civilized because in the religion class at school, we had learned that they weren't. We were told we had to get rid of those "uncivilized" practices our grandparents adhered to. To my generation, they were "way back!"

Moreover, Grandma used supplications and affirmations in her world, asking the universe to be clement and provide the abundance her family needed. I witnessed this especially during the drought when Grandma would say her supplications to ask for rain. Another time was when Mother Nature was angry and sent us hailstones; Grandma burned some type of animal skin (I don't even know what it was, but it smelled awful), and put it in front of our house to make the hail go away. It wasn't much about what she burnt, but what she intended in that gesture.

Health-wise, my grandmother performed colon cleansings for herself and her grandkids whom she raised, using herbs and other medicinal plants. She would try to heal all my wounds and other booboos even if sometimes it didn't work. Come to think of it now, I can see that Grandma was ahead of her time.

Uncle Apollinaire must have known more about education and modern civilization than his mother. He had joined the army right after sixth grade, which was all it took to be admitted. He had earned the rank of corporal, which wasn't high, but he was known as a *muzungu* ("white person" in Kirundi). People in the villages didn't think there was any distinction between being well off and being a white person, so they saw my uncle as being the same as a white man. His military career afforded him a better life than most in the village. He could send his parents some money for rice at Christmas, and use a very good smelling soap called Lux that I liked so much. It also allowed him to marry a southern belle whose beauty was breathtaking.

Melanie was eighteen years old when she married Uncle Apollinaire, while he was in his late thirties. She and I quickly became friends. As I grew older, I was the one she confided in more than my aunts, and she always treated me well and brought me treats after she'd been to the market. She used to tell me that she wished I could marry her cousin John who was a high school senior at that time. Although I entertained the fantasy in my pre-teen mind, her cousin was way older than me, but to Melanie, that wasn't a problem. I was protective of my uncle's wife. Because we were close, we went for errands together, and each time a man made a pass at her (and God knows men did), I would give him a disgusted look, and Melanie always thanked me. She had her share of marital difficulties that I didn't understand much about at the time, but my grandmother was always a good mother-in-law to her. She treated Melanie as one of her own children. And because Uncle Apollinaire was her only son, Grandma sometimes unintentionally favored Melanie over her own daughters.

My uncle put me in school because he had a vision of what it meant to be an educated person. Even though I didn't understand the importance of education at the time, and I sometimes preferred my grandmother's sweet plans, I came to appreciate what he did for me later. He paid for my primary education up to sixth grade. That's all I needed to get through and beat the system. Had I been in the care of my own parents, I would have ended up like my two older sisters, either voluntarily quitting school like Claire, or worse, being withdrawn from school by my parents to help them on the farm, as they had done with my oldest sister Eugenie. Eugenie had been first in her class from first to fifth grade, but she had been pulled out of school by my parents to help my mother with domestic work and raise her siblings. Unlike Claire, who was given many chances to repeat sixth grade, but pulled herself out of school (because boys bothered her, she said), my sister Eugenie loved school, but was not given the chance.

Uncle Apollinaire only had the financial means to put me through primary school, which consisted of grades one through six. In sixth grade, we had to pass a national exam that assessed our admission into high school. In our class, I was one of the four students who passed the test out of approximately fifty students who had taken it. Even though passing this exam was a big deal in a kid's life, and I should have been excited, I was worried. Who was going to pay the high school tuition? It couldn't be Uncle Apollinaire. He had just retired from his military career, so he had no money to pay for my high school.

The locations of boarding schools where we would be sent were announced a month before the school year began. We had two months of summer vacation that I was supposed to enjoy since I had passed the national exam. But I kept asking myself, "Am I really going to high school? Who is going to pay for it and which school will I be sent to?"

That year, my beloved grandmother, who had raised me, died, and everything changed. Aunt Aurelia had married, and Barenga, my adopted aunt, had also met her beau. I had shifted to being a caregiver to my grandparents long before Grandma died. Her health had deteriorated so much that I became the one Grandma and Grandpa relied on. Officially, my uncle's wife Melanie and I were in charge. But my grandmother never wanted to burden her daughter-in-law, so she turned to me for her care. She had battled her asthma for so long, and one day, she just stopped breathing. I only have selective memories of the day she died, probably because that is how I coped with her death.

All I remember is that Barenga had spent the night at our house. The next day around noon, she came home from the fields to have lunch. Although Barenga was married and had a home of her own, she always came to help my grandmother with farm work. When she went to check on Grandma, I heard her scream. She had found my grandmother cold and breathless on her bed. I never went in my grandmother's room to look at her body. It was a good thing because to this day, I only have memories of my grandmother alive and not dead. My cousin and I were sent off to tell our two maternal aunts, Scholastica and Aurelia, who lived seven hours' walking distance away. Since we had no telephones, it was the only way we could communicate their mother's death. When we got to Aunt Aurelia's house, before we could tell her the reason for our unannounced visit, I burst out crying; Aunt Aurelia immediately knew what had happened. She understood how I felt because Grandma had practically been the only mother I truly knew.

Although I visited my paternal grandparents during the holidays when I was in elementary school, I wasn't as close to them as I was to my maternal grandparents. My dad's father suffered from an illness I didn't understand at the time. Whenever I visited him, he never recognized me. My paternal grandmother, Regina, would tell him, "Daoudi, Sekunda has come to visit us." But my grandfather only stared at her. Then she would repeat, "Sekunda, Gaspard's daughter, she is here to greet you!" But he never seemed to understand. Grandpa Daoudi was a strongly built man. Looking at his physical appearance, no one would have suspected that he wasn't well. He was tall, with strong leg muscles, and was very attractive for a Grandpa!

I kind of felt hurt because I was used to the attention of my maternal grandparents, and this granddaddy wasn't excited to see me; he didn't even know who I was! I gave up on getting his attention; I figured that my other grandfather would never ignore me. But, of course, Grandpa Daoudi wasn't ignoring me. He was the same with his other grand-kids who lived on the same compound with him and played around him every day. He still didn't know any of them, and he always seemed withdrawn and far away. No one in my family ever understood what was wrong with him, but everyone seemed to accept it as an incurable condition. It is only now that I think back and realize he probably suffered from Alzheimer's disease, which might have claimed his life.

Despite her health issues, my maternal grandmother lived a long life, full of love for those around her. I missed her love, which would follow me into my adult years when I would look for love in the wrong places. I was once again prematurely severed from my loved ones, and it seemed no one understood what I was going through. I kept the pain to myself so I would not appear too needy for love and affection. After my grandmother's death, my grandfather became sicker and weaker by the day. He died three years after.

CHAPTER 5 EVOLVING QUESTIONS FOR REFLECTION

1. Losing my grandmother was the first time I experienced the death of someone I loved so much. What is a situation that has affected you in a painful way?

_____

_____

_____

_____

_____

2. What did you learn from that situation?

_____

_____

_____

_____

_____

3. How might you use what you learned then to help yourself and those around you today?

_____

_____

_____

_____

_____

Chapter 6

GETTING SHIPPED BACK HOME

Give a little love to a child, and you get a great deal back.
—John Ruskin

Now that I had passed the national exam and Uncle Apollinaire realized he wasn't able to pay for my high school tuition, he made a decision. From now on, I was to be handed back to my real parents, Gaspard and Suzanne. They would decide whether I would go on to high school or if I would stay home, work on the farm, and hence, get married without underwear or a bra! That certainly wasn't what I wanted. So, I returned to live with my parents with some apprehension. *Oh, God, please, I want to be wearing underwear when I get married.* Wearing underwear to me had a sense of security, a protection for my private parts. Although I wore it when I started school, along with my blue skirt and white blouse school uniform, only rich kids could wear decent underwear. And wearing it at my wedding was even more important because I felt that then my husband would take his time to unwrap me—one piece of clothing at a time. Certainly, the stories I had heard from Barenga and her girlfriends were giving me scary thoughts about marriage and sex.

Unless I was studying to become the next president of Burundi, my father considered school a waste of precious farming time. Although I had passed the national exam qualifying me for high school, my dad wasn't anxious about how I would pay the tuition because he didn't intend to send me to high school. He never understood why my brothers and I were in school, something he had never needed to do as the oldest son in his own family. He would tell us kids that we were in school just to escape the home chores (which at least in my case was true). "I didn't go to school. What do you need school for—to be president?" my father would say. I suspect that maybe Dad regretted not having gone to school. In my teenage mind, I felt he had tried to escape the farm work himself when he went to East Africa to seek work in Tanzania and Uganda in the early 1970s. I wanted to tell him that, but I knew better, so I kept quiet.

Until that time, I had never "met" my dad in person. When I had visited my family while I still lived with my grandparents, he was still in Tanzania. I had left home before I was old enough to form memories of him in my mind. Although people said we looked alike, I didn't even know whether I would recognize him if we met. At some point, my father was believed dead because we stopped getting news of him, especially during the war of 1972. After the war, my uncle Isidore, one of my father's younger brothers, had gone to Tanzania to look for him, but he didn't find him. Before I met my father, I fantasized a lot about him. I imagined him as a fun-loving, caring man, who would bring us so many nice things, like dresses and shoes when he would come home from Kampala and Dar es Salaam. That's where I had heard grownups say he had been seen the last time someone gave us his news. We were not even exactly sure in which city in East Africa he lived.

Years later, all my idolizing of my father was proven to be wrong. He disappointed me in every way. He came back home with no dresses, no shoes for me or my sisters, nothing for my three brothers either. In brief, he came back with nothing to show for his long absence. My mom had stepped in and become mom and dad, raising the kids alone. She had enrolled my two older brothers Emmanuel and Cyriaque in school. She tended to the crops and sold grains in summer to raise elementary school tuition for my brothers. At one point, she had to sell a cow to raise enough money to send both boys to school and to provide for the whole family. When my dad returned from East Africa, my mother never questioned his efforts or what he had been doing the whole time. Then she told him how she had handled the family during his time away, and that she had had to sell a cow so she could send the boys to school. Father wasn't pleased with this announcement. He started resenting us kids for asking him to pay school tuition. On nights when he had had a few too many, he would come home late at night and start an argument out of nowhere insulting my mother and even beating her in front of us. At that time, I wished our mother could stand up for herself, but she just crashed under the abuse. Sometimes, my older siblings had to get involved in the fight to defend her. I was always scared and retreated into a corner away from the rest. I would block my ears, hoping not to hear the fights going on in my home. I never said a word, and my father sometimes praised me as the sweet child for not challenging him about his behavior like my older siblings did. I suppose I was trying to get into his good graces so he wouldn't hurt me. I just wished school would resume so I could escape before I got hurt. Basically, school was my escape from my home's turmoil, and there was no alternative for me but to succeed in school.

Dad's temper always deteriorated around the time school began again. He didn't want to hear another word about school supplies or tuition money. Therefore, when it was time for me to go to high school, I didn't know who would pay for it. I was terrified to ask him for anything. My mother kept pressuring him to find a solution, which only aggravated him. I would hear him say, "Why can't she stay home and farm like other girls in this village? What's so special about her that she needs to go to high school, to become a government minister or what?" (He had lowered the standard from president).

Here I was, finally living with my real family for good, but I didn't really fit in. Before, I had only visited my family during major holidays, and I had always felt like a special guest. Whenever I visited, it was like being in another state for a sightseeing occasion, so I didn't have to adapt to the culture. And it felt like another culture. My family even teased me about my accent because slight differences existed in how people from the lower landscapes talked compared to those from the highlands. So, when I went to live permanently with my parents, my siblings always annoyed me by commenting on each word I said. They would correct me and make me repeat the "right and proper way" to say a word.

The other thing my siblings, and sometimes my parents, complained about was that I was a very spoiled child, and that had to do with my crying. Whenever they teased me, I cried, and then they would tease me more, and I would cry more! Also, they complained about my labor hours. I wasn't necessarily good at farming with the hoe, and if I could, I would have avoided it altogether. But I had to do my share. Since they could see that I didn't like it, they would complain some more and I would cry some more. I remember one day my father told me to hold a little calf so he could milk its mother. He knew I didn't like holding calves. They moved a lot, and once I had been hurt by a calf at my grandparents' house. The little cow's leg had bruised my ankle, and the bruise had turned into an infection that took months to heal. In my mind, I had made the decision to avoid holding baby cows while their mother was being milked. Calves are hyper; they just want to rush to drink their mother's milk. However, that day, my father put me to the task of holding the calf, and I made a terrible mistake and said, "No." Attitude!

My father made me hold the little cow anyway, and then he said, "I'll see how many cows you bring me when you get married." He was referring to the custom of a man paying his future wife's family a dowry in cows. And the number of cows, as well as how fat they were, determined how much value the husband's family placed on you as their son's future wife.

When in my parents' care, I longed to be with my sweet grandmother. I found the strife in my family exhausting. I was used to living with my elderly grandparents, who no longer had anything to fight about. My siblings seemed to notice that I wasn't enjoying living with them, and they never tired of teasing me about it, which only made me feel lonelier. It seemed as if no one could understand my feelings. They certainly didn't miss my dead Grandma as much as I did. I didn't know what to do to belong fully to this family.

Everyone in my family also seemed to be braver than me. For instance, at night, each of my brothers and sisters could go by him- or herself to the bathroom (built outside) but I couldn't. Because of the killings in 1972 that had severely affected my hometown, I was frightened to go outside at night by myself. Usually, I would ask my oldest sister, Eugenie, to accompany me and she did. But if I had been a bad girl that day or disrespectful to her, my punishment came at night; then she would refuse to go with me when I needed to go to the bathroom. And I knew better than to ask my bossy sister Claire. I couldn't ask my two older brothers because they were boys, and I was a girl; boundaries had to be enforced. I couldn't ask my two younger siblings either because they were too young.

One night, I really had to go and I had to show these people what I was made of! Gathering my courage, I ventured out by myself to go to the toilet. As soon as I set foot outside, my heart jumped in my throat. The banana trees became —tall, mean men, wearing long, ugly, brown coats, and huge ugly, black old cowboy hats. They seemed to hold spears in their hands, but I couldn't see well. My family heard me wrestling with the door, trying to get back inside, but I felt a backward pull by the bad guys who certainly had followed me to the house. By the time I made it inside, everyone, including my mother, who was otherwise very quiet, exploded with laugher. Out of breath and with wild eyes, I tried to explain what I had just seen, only to cause my siblings to laugh uproariously until their stomachs hurt. Then I felt humiliated that I had lacked the courage to go outside at night by myself, even this once. That's all I needed —a one-time courageous moment to beat the demons of fear.

Out of pity, my sister Eugenie took me back outside to do my business. She asked me to show her what I had seen. But, of course, the banana trees had regained their original shape, and no bad guys wearing ugly long coats and hats were in sight. We just laughed about the silliness of it all. Eugenie told me no bad guys had been outside, since the war of 1972—that it was all my imagination. Her wise words were lost on me because I remained scared to go outside alone at night. Little did I know that out of all seven children, I would be the one who would end up flying far…far away from home!

CHAPTER 6 EVOLVING QUESTIONS FOR REFLECTION

1. Describe your relationship with your parents.

_____

_____

_____

_____

_____

2. What was your relationship with your siblings or other family members when you were growing up?

_____

_____

_____

_____

_____

3. What did they teach you that helped you become who you are today?

_____

_____

_____

_____

_____

Chapter 7

TAKING THE HIGH ROAD TO HIGH SCHOOL

The roots of education are bitter, but the fruit is sweet.
—Aristotle

That summer of 1980, I had been looking forward to knowing what boarding school the Department of Education would enroll me in. By mid-August, the results of who passed the sixth grade national exam, the scores, and the schools where students had been assigned were announced. The results were posted on bulletin boards at every major elementary school district. I went to look for my name and found that I had been enrolled in the Lycée of Gisanze, a girls only boarding high school. I had never heard of that school before. It was located in the province of Muyinga, at the border of northern Burundi and southern Rwanda. Given my humble beginnings, traveling from my hometown to the school was going to be a huge impediment, if I even went to school. Even for those who had money, traveling from the south all the way to the north end of the country was a challenge due to the lack of transportation and good roads.

After I told my parents what school I had been assigned to, my father was indifferent because he knew I wasn't going anywhere.

Who was going to pay for it? As far as he was concerned, I had exceeded all expectations in education. I had achieved sixth grade level, and that was more than enough for a girl. On my dad's side, we had a university graduate, my youngest uncle, Vincent, who had graduated from a university in the now former Union of Soviet Socialist Republics in Moscow. He was my hero even though I had not seen him yet. That's because he came every once in a-while for vacations, and each time he had come home, I had been in school and still living with my grandparents. His vacations never coincided with mine. But I always heard that we had a very smart uncle in Moscow. I felt I had to go as far in school as my uncle had. However, because I wasn't a boy, I knew there would be limitations. That dream of mine was far more achievable for my two brothers Emmanuel and Cyriaque, both in ninth grade at the time. They were boys and likely to further their education. So far, they were proving all expectations right. Uncle Vincent had been paying for their high school tuition.

Each time I asked my dad whether I would go to high school, he looked unconcerned, but I could tell he didn't have a plan. Moreover, he was too proud to ask his younger brother Vincent whether he could pay for my tuition too, since he was already paying for my two brothers. My other paternal uncles had many kids as well, and it seemed as if we all counted on Uncle Vincent's kindness to pay our tuition, for those of us who went beyond sixth grade. Not knowing what to do with me, since I wasn't good at farming with the hoe, my father finally asked my uncle whether he would pay for my tuition, so I could go to high school. Uncle Vincent accepted, God bless his heart.

The lycée where I was assigned for my high school studies was far away from my hometown. It took two days of traveling, but that was under normal circumstances. The distance between my hometown and my school town is approximately six hundred miles. By Western standards, that distance is easily travelled on the highway system. No one in my family knew where the school was located, and no one volunteered to take me there. Under normal circumstances again, my dad would have been the one to accompany me to boarding school. But if he did, it would have taken two bus tickets, or should I say two truck tickets? The country didn't have many buses at the time; nor could my family afford the bus fare. My parents were struggling to send me on a one way trip to the lycée, and they didn't have a plan for how I would return home for vacations. We would worry about that later.

Transportation consisted of commercial trucks, or sometimes, pickups would travel to Bujumbura, the capital of Burundi and major city. From there, I would have to be loaded on another truck that linked Bujumbura to the province of Ngozi's city center, before reaching my destination, in the province of Muyinga. The school was located in a remote village where missionaries had come since colonial times. There was one primary school, one high school (the lycée), one Catholic church, and one small outdoor market place.

The part I looked forward to on that trip was seeing the capital for the first time. That's what I liked about this long distance boarding school event. After that, I had no idea where I would go or how. Going to Bujumbura was going to be relatively easy since Uncle Vincent worked in the capital. That part of the trip was not going to be a problem and he had agreed to pay for my ticket there. The road trip from Bujumbura to the school was still an issue, and my mother kept pressing my father to figure it out. Like another miracle sent by God, my mom suddenly thought of Ananias, the pastor. What an "Aha!" moment Mother had! Ananias, our neighbor, was a Protestant pastor working as an evangelist in the province of Muyinga, trying to instill some Christianity into the people of a remote village. His preaching office was approximately forty miles by bike from where my school was. He had just come for his summer vacation to visit his family who lived across the valley from our house. Ananias was a man much known for his kindness, Christian religious teachings, and good heart. So, my mom went to Ananias' house to tell him about my situation, and ask for guidance. She got blessings instead. Not only did Ananias know where the school was located, but he offered to take me there in person. Hallelujah, praise the Lord!

Here I was, starting a new chapter of my life, going six hundred miles away from home, to a remote school village where modern civilization was still being introduced to people. It would be reported to me later that the region was better known for werewolves, witchcraft, and other black magic activities I have forced myself to forget over time. But because Ananias was going to take me to school, I stopped worrying for a while. As if I had a lucky charm, his vacation ended the same time as mine, so we hit the road a week before school was due to begin. The plan was to go to Ananias' preaching village first, and stay there for a couple of days, waiting for school to start. In the meantime, I would be acquainting myself with the area. Then he would take me to school on his bike. Let me tell you something: it is one thing to ride a bike in your neighborhood, but when it's your only means of transportation to boarding school for forty miles, it's no fun. I didn't even know how to ride a bike. Ananias was going to be in charge of riding the bike, balancing my life on his backseat.

The day Ananias and I met to start our journey for my high school adventure, we got a free car ride to Bujumbura. Ananias was well known in the community, and the few rich people in my village who had cars knew him. They all happened to be Protestants and businessmen, and he was their pastor. They would have driven him anywhere if he'd asked, but he wasn't a man who took advantage of others. When we arrived in Bujumbura at night, the city glowed! It was my imagined paradise. Lights at night make any city look glorious and glamorous. I was to be housed at the home of my dad's second cousin (maybe once removed). No, there is no such thing as "removed" cousins in Burundi; family is family no matter how many generations apart. And you don't want them removed; you might need them to house your fifth child who's going to high school by herself.

I spent the night at my dad's cousin's house in awe. There were so many firsts for me. First time I had been in a fancy house with bedrooms, and doors on each room! First time I saw fancy kids with shoes and pressed clothes. First time I saw a toilet seat in white ceramic and inside the house! My dad's cousin's wife asked me smart questions, and I tried to give smart answers. Ananias went to spend the night somewhere else with his Protestant friends, where they probably spent the night praying (and I was sure he'd be praying for me without even being asked); he was such a committed evangelist.

The next day, Ananias and I had to hit the road again. In the morning, he came to pick me up, and we took the bus to the central market where the action was. It seemed to be the center of the universe. The central market in many African capital cities is where major economical activities happen. The transportation, shopping, foreign currency transactions, noise, pick-pockets— everybody was busy doing something, or going somewhere. All the merchants had outdoor stalls, and their radios were as loud as possible so the music would attract customers' attention. And the chaos —oh my goodness, I loved it! This is what you miss when you grow up in a village.

We took a bus called "*hiace.*" It's the size of a ten-person mini-van, not exactly as fancy, but it could transport more than twenty people on a non-busy day. Thank God we didn't have to take one of those big merchandise transportation trucks in which you couldn't see where you were going that we called "*Tugezehe,*" literally meaning "*Are we there yet?*" Those trucks belonged to big Arab merchants or other rich businessmen. They were packed to the roof, and people were loaded on top of the merchandise. The main roads connecting Bujumbura to the province city centers were paved, and not too dusty. However, once we got off the main national roads (the equivalent of highways I suppose), roads were bumpy, and dusty to boot.

So, it was really glamorous only up to the province of Ngozi's city center. Once in Ngozi, we took link transportation—this time a pickup. But the driver and two other people who paid first class fare rode inside the pickup. The rest of us, who purchased economy coach, rode in the back. And because the pickup had steel bars that allowed passengers to hold on, we were packed to maximize the return on investment of the Toyota pickup. Pastor Ananias rode inside the truck because he could afford it. He looked at me from his front seat through the glass window, and I could see pain in his eyes. He was probably wondering how my parents dared to send me to such a far-away land and not send anyone with me on this first journey. I saw the look on his face, but I made it a point not to cry. Even though I felt a need to release emotions, I wasn't going to be a cry-baby on my journey to being a high school student. *I had to grow up or else.*

I focused on the good I would reap one day. First, how I would grow taller, so when I went home for the Christmas holidays, everybody would be amazed by how much I had grown in just three months! Then I fantasized about how I would go to church on

Sundays, and all eyes would turn to me because that's what happened to high school or university students. After Sunday Mass, the crowd would just surround you and stare at you as if you were an alien, only cuter. I knew it would happen to me when I would go to church during the holidays. I could already feel the stares, and some gossiping whispers. Because I didn't grow up in my hometown, many people didn't know who I was, except some relatives. Therefore, people at church would ask who I was and try to figure it out through my sisters with whom I went to church. This reaction always made me feel like an outcast right in my own hometown. The stares were annoying sometimes because people would check you out and talk on and on in whispers. But on that journey going to the pastor's house in Muyinga, I focused on the good, if only to avoid crying.

After we reached our destination, we walked about two miles to the pastor's house. As soon as we arrived, Ananias made sure he ordered his housekeeper to feed me as if to compensate for the days I hadn't eaten healthy food in the past, and the days I wouldn't be eating healthy food in the future. But I couldn't eat anything. I just couldn't swallow food. The fancy bread, tea with milk and sugar for breakfast in the morning, and the good lunches and dinners prepared for pastors were all wasted on me. All I could have wished for in a meal was there, but I couldn't get myself to eat. My heart was so heavy, and I felt a need to cry, but I didn't dare in Ananias' presence. He kept pressing me to eat, but I couldn't.

Ananias kept reminding me how important this education was for me and my parents. He said there weren't many educated girls in our hometown, so it was important that I eat to be healthy and strong, and go to school and study hard. But why me? Why did I have to be the hero for educated girls in my hometown? Why did I have to be the one going to foreign territories? Suddenly, I longed for what my grandmother used to say: had I just gone to catechism school, I'd be long done with school now. I had exceeded expectations (and I had underwear) so, why did I need the non-sense and trauma of high school? But here I was, and seemingly, Ananias wasn't going to let me escape. He had brought me this far, and his Christian religious beliefs encouraged him to seek a better life, so he understood the importance of education, while my own father didn't. Sometimes, I had wondered whether being Catholic wasn't a setback for my family. All our Protestant neighbors seemed to understand the importance of seeking a better life for their families; and they were always successful in business. The Protestant men didn't drink alcohol, whereas some of the Catholic men drank too much, which in some cases was accompanied by battering their wives. Protestant families also seemed to live in well-built homes, when compared to Catholic families—at least those I knew at that particular time.

The day Ananias and I were to leave for my final arrival to the boarding school, he readied his bicycle. He tied my luggage on it, sat me back on the seat, and sat in front of me. Then he told me, "Sweetheart, you have to hold really tight on my back so you won't fall." Okay, so there was this possibility that I might actually fall into the street while going to high school? Well, I held as tightly as I could. I held on for dear life while traveling the bumpy streets of that remote village. He rode until his forehead started dropping beads of sweat. He rode until his back, which I was holding, became soaked with sweat. But he continued to ride the forty miles on bike without taking a break. And we made it! We got to the school the afternoon before everybody else was due to arrive. Ananias had wisely decided that I would arrive at school a day early, to get accustomed to the nuns who ran the school.

We introduced ourselves to the nuns. Ananias explained to Sister Marie, the headmistress, why I was early, and he gave her his contact information as my guardian angel if there were anything to report about me. I hoped there wouldn't be any problem in my case, unless my school tuition wasn't paid. Where would I then be sent in order to be shipped back home? To Ananias's house, of course. Fortunately, everything had been paid for that first quarter; I just needed to put my little brain to work and get through that first term. Sister Marie was a beautiful and tall nun. She wore a long dress which hung slightly below her knees, a pullover, a nun's veil, and open sandals, all white. She looked very much together and in command, and I instantly felt I could both trust her and fear her authority. I learned later she was very strict as well. She introduced me to the head matron, Sister Helen, another tall nun who was the head of dormitory affairs, food matters, and everything related to the school's logistics. And this was no small job, considering that the lycée housed close to five hundred girls from grades 7 to 13. Sister Helen had to be even stricter, so I made up my mind that I would have to be on my best behavior. She showed me to a room where I would spend the night in the convent's guest house. Thank God they didn't want me sleeping in the dormitory alone before others arrived. It would have been really scary. I was grateful that Sister Helen let me stay in the convent.

When it was time for my guardian angel Ananias to leave, my eyes started burning with acid tears. This was the worst goodbye moment I had ever had in my life. As soon as he announced his leaving, a stream of tears filled my eyes. All the tears I had been holding back for days, since leaving home, were now spilling out. I didn't want him to leave me. I cried a river of tears that refused to drain. I didn't know where the tears were coming from, and I tried to compose myself, reasoning that after all, this man was only a good Samaritan and not my father. But I couldn't stop crying. Ananias tried to lecture me about the importance of education again— how it was in my best interest to stay and learn—but the tears kept running down my cheeks, regardless, and when I tried to stop crying, the terrible sobs that took over and shook me were even worse. Sister Marie tried her best to console me. She ordered warm milk with sugar for me, but I couldn't drink it or swallow. And when I made an effort for the nun's sake, my stomach couldn't keep it down, so I stopped trying. I was a mess.

Eventually, Ananias had to leave. Like a mother trying to separate herself from a toddler on the first day of daycare, he had to turn away and just leave me there without looking back. He had to return to his evangelical job. He had a mission in life, so he couldn't just stay there and babysit me. The sisters assured him that I would be fine once other students started coming. Ananias, seemingly shocked as well, gathered his courage, and left me there with the nuns. I cried until I was dehydrated.

Later that evening, three seventh graders came to spend the night. Then, because we were four, the nuns let us sleep in the dormitory where seventh graders would be sleeping. I was ecstatic! This was a school after all, and not just a nun's place—other kids would come here to study! All my tears dried away and all my anxiety vanished. They were replaced by a sense of relief and hope.

We went to make our beds, but the other girls did not know how. I am proud to say that I was the savvier one. They were accompanied by their dads, of course—lucky them. One of the girls' dads helped her make her bed. First, he put the blanket on the bed and then the sheets on top. But this was not a warm region, so I didn't think he did it on purpose. The girl was embarrassed, but out of respect, she didn't tell her dad that he had made the bed upside down. I was envious of her that at least her dad was with her and making an effort to help her get settled in a boarding school. I had been trained in making beds by Melanie, Uncle Apollinaire's wife. They had a modern bed, with mattress and sheets, of course. She had taught me how to make a bed, insisting that I had to know for when I would have a husband. It became my job to make their bed every day because when my uncle was away, I slept with Melanie. But I was kicked out whenever he came home for vacations. I slept with Barenga instead, in my grandparents' house, on the floor where we laid thick grass for cushioning. But as soon as Uncle Apollinaire left, I went back to sleep with Melanie on their modern bed.

As at any good school for girls only, the sisters trained us how to make our beds properly. They also taught us good manners, including the proper way to wash ourselves—you know, girl parts and all that. They taught us about menstruation (thanks to Barenga, I had been given a heads up on the subject) and how to wear feminine pads for those of us who didn't know yet. This was definitely a fine girls' school. That first night in the boarding school, I slept like a baby (probably because I was exhausted from crying). It would be the first of many happy nights and no more crying until the Christmas holiday when we went home for vacations.

We had a two-week break each Christmas. My first Christmas during my high school, the plan was that my family would send me a ticket for the transportation fare, using postal money orders, so I could go back and visit them. At the lycée, there was a custom on the Friday preceding the return home for holiday breaks. It was a money orders day. All the students were gathered in front of the dormitories, and names were called for those who got money orders. That Friday, when the nun in charge started calling names, my name didn't get called. I hoped to be next, or next, or maybe next…but no! Almost every kid in seventh grade got a money order except me. I didn't cry. Oh no, I was a big girl now! But mostly, I didn't cry because I kept expecting money for some reason, without knowing who was going to be my next Samaritan. Friday afternoon gave way to Saturday morning and my money order still hadn't come. All the students were to leave on Saturday around 10 a.m. so I started to fear the worst. Where was I going to be when everybody would climb the school pickup truck to go home? I didn't have any idea. My mind raced with possibilities, but I refused to consider that I wouldn't be going home.

When it was almost time for students to leave school, Sister Helen came to my dorm and called me. Whew! My money had come, praise the Lord! I finally had a return home ticket for Christmas vacation like the other kids. Two thousand Burundi francs (the equivalent of two U.S. dollars) was wealth to me at that time, although today it would buy almost nothing. I checked the sender section on the money order to find out who had sent me the money. Who else than my beloved Uncle Vincent? It was the happiest moment of my life. I, too, was going home to my family. It seemed as if God had worked out some wonders again. My parents never could have afforded a ticket to bring me home for the holidays and send me back to school in only two weeks. I was to go from the Lycée of Gisanze to Bujumbura for transition, and then from Bujumbura to Vugizo, my hometown.

I was certainly looking forward to going home to show off how many inches taller I had grown, and how much weight I had gained. Yeah, believe me, I wanted to gain weight back then! Except for my behind, my little body was small. But my behind was oversized in proportion to my body frame, and that followed me from primary school to…well, all my life practically; until I learned that a big behind was an asset and not a liability. In Africa, curves are regarded as an attractive feature in the same way big boobs are in the

American culture (the difference being that you can't have a butt implant or maybe you can!) Anyway, I expected some growth and weight gain, and I couldn't wait to go home and be checked out by the onlookers after Sunday Mass.

Since the morning the holidays started, wealthy parents who had cars had been coming to pick up their kids. Some students in the senior grades (twelve and thirteen) who had wealthy boyfriends with cars were picked up as well. But the vast majority of us paid for our own transportation. It consisted of the school pickup truck, courtesy of the lycée, packing as many students aboard as it could. The school pickup drove students and dropped them off at a junction road between Muyinga and Kirundo provinces, where the traffic flowed more frequently. Priority was given to those who lived the farthest from the school, which meant all the students from farther south in the province of Bururi. From that junction, students then took whatever had wheels to Ngozi city center. Once in Ngozi, we rushed to climb on the mini-buses to Bujumbura. After Bujumbura, I still had to take connecting transportation to Vugizo.

I was excited to ride with the other students and not miss any of the fun. I was so ready for any mischief that would come my way on that school pickup. The girls' chanting had already begun. As I started climbing into the back of the school pickup truck, I saw Pastor Ananias approaching on his bike. *The bike?* Oh God, not the bike again! I panicked. Why was he here? What was the problem? Didn't he get the memo that this was the happiest, wildest moment in my youth? I was going home after three months of absence to see my family. He approached the school pickup and spoke to one of the teachers, Mr. Menard, who taught in the upper grades and happened to be from my hometown. Ananias told him that he had come to take me to his home in Muyinga to spend the Christmas holidays with him because I was too young to travel home and come back to school alone. When Mr. Menard told me to step down out of the pickup truck and go with the pastor, I refused. Then, before I could blink, my eyes were spilling burning tears along my cheeks. Between my tears and a broken trembling voice, I told Ananias, "I received the ticket from my uncle, and he is expecting me to go home and I want to go home." He reasoned with me for some time, and the Toyota pickup was about to leave without me. My friends were going home. Why not me? I threw a big seventh grade tantrum. Then both men realized how upset I was, and Mr. Menard persuaded the pastor to let me go home, offering to chaperone me. Convinced that I would be in Mr. Menard's good hands, Pastor Ananias let me go home. All my friends were happy for me as I climbed back in the pickup. We left and didn't waste any time singing our wildest songs. Where did these girls learn all those songs? The songs were filled with words we wouldn't necessarily say in front of our parents. I realized that some of the girls had been involved in extra-curricular activities.

As we hurried to board the crowded mini-buses in Ngozi's city center, Mr. Menard made sure I was still among the crowd. We took our bus to Bujumbura where we arrived in the night. Again, when I saw it from the upper hills of Ijenda when approaching the capital, Bujumbura glowed. My heart soared with pride for my country's beautiful city of light. Although I could have gone to dad's second cousin's house to spend the night, I didn't know how to get there and it was late. So Mr. Menard decided I would go with him to spend the night where he was going.

We went to a poor neighborhood with squalid houses that was, and still is, a major prostitute's quarter. Mr. Menard spent the night doing R- rated stuff with the hookers who lived in the house. I didn't sleep that night at all; I was kind of scared of Mr. Menard now. I tried to reason in my seventh grade mind that grownups were entitled to have sex, but I didn't appreciate that Mr. Menard, a teacher I respected, did it with hookers, and while I was in the same house. In addition, the heat and the mosquitoes made the night too long, painful, and ugly. But I kept my spirits up because I knew that the next day I would see my family. I couldn't wait for the day to come.

The next day, Mr. Menard came to wake me up at six in the morning. He looked dehydrated (or was it my imagination?). We went to the central market where we took transportation home.

My parents and siblings were happy to see me. And yes, they confirmed that I had grown taller. In our immediate family, we were not meant to be tall, so I was doing my part as best as I could. Two weeks went by fast, but it was the best vacation ever spent with my family. My siblings said my accent had changed yet again. They said I now spoke with a Kinyarwanda (Rwandan language) accent. Because of my school's proximity to Rwanda, there were a lot of Rwandan students at the school, and four of the nuns who ran the school, as well as some of the teachers, were Rwandans, so it's possible that my accent had really changed. After the two weeks holidays ended, going back to school presented other challenges I hadn't foreseen.

I left on the day the holidays ended to go to Bujumbura. That part presented no problems. The next day, I took the bus to Ngozi's city center. I spent the night at the home of Uncle Vincent's friend, a military officer whom my uncle had asked to help me in Ngozi. The plan was that my uncle's friend would put me on the bus to Muyinga the next day. There was no straight transportation to Gisanze, the remote village where my school was located. That's why the school had arranged to pick students up at a main intersection between the road to Gisanze and the road to the center of Muyinga province. This arrangement ran only on the first day of school. If you were not there on the specific day at the specific time, the school pickup would never see you, and you would never meet your school pickup either. And the driver never saw me because I went there the second day of school, since I had left my hometown on the last day of the vacations. The day I was supposed to get on the school pickup was the one I spent in Ngozi.

The army officer who housed me in Ngozi went to the market with me the next morning. He put me on the bus to Muyinga with the understanding that I would have to get off at the intersection where I should have been the day before to get on the school pickup. I knew I would not be meeting any school pickup there, so I had to walk to school from that intersection. It was about fifteen miles that I had to walk, nothing to worry about, I was used to walking since elementary school. I don't know exactly what time I got there, but it was early afternoon, so, I was not afraid that I would have to walk in the night. I didn't have any heavy bags, only my little bag of a few belongings, and my tuition money that Uncle Vincent had given me for the second trimester. So I had to hold on tight to this money and not lose it.

After I got off the bus to Muyinga at the right intersection, I started walking along the one road to the school. The road was surrounded by high bushes and trees. But I didn't have the luxury of thinking scary thoughts because I had to walk fast. On my way, I met people going about their daily business, but each one of the men I met carried a machete in his hand. Now, a machete is a cutting tool, so I thought maybe they were going to cut trees or grass or whatever. But because in 1972 during the civil war, machetes were used to kill Tutsis, I didn't feel safe meeting these people carrying machetes. In addition, Muyinga, the province where my school was located, was one of the most affected by the wars of 1972 and 1973 and was a Hutu majority province. Furthermore,

I remembered the myths about there being people in that region who turned into werewolves after sunset. I consider this a myth now, but it was a scary myth when you are a seventh grader; life is too sweet to be eaten by werewolves.

Perhaps because of my fear of being killed by those machete holders or eaten if they changed into animals, I must have released my mighty grip on the handkerchief in which I had wrapped my tuition money into a small knot. My total wealth consisted of that tuition money, and a little extra cash for my living expenses for the second trimester, all wrapped in a pretty white hanky I had bought for that purpose. Now it was gone! But I couldn't walk back to look for it, could I? After walking for a while, I stopped worrying that someone was going to eat me; I wasn't that good or chubby. I then realized for real that I had lost my money.

"My money—the money Uncle Vincent gave me! Oh my God, I lost my tuition money!" I freaked out for a few seconds, and then I told myself: "Stay calm, stay calm." And miraculously, I did calm down. I usually cried in every other situation, but I never cried in a difficult situation like this. I turned and started going back the way I had come, looking on the ground to try to see where I had dropped my money. I didn't care anymore about meeting bad guys because I had lost my tuition money; I had to find it. I kept walking faster, looking on the ground with all the mighty vision I had been given, trying to use my intuition to locate where I might have loosened my grip and dropped the money. I tried to walk as fast as I could, almost jogging.

After twenty minutes or so of walking back, I saw a man holding a machete in his hand, walking in my direction. Immediately, I turned back, this time walking toward the school where I was supposed to be going in the first place. I gave up on the money because the man kept making signs to me, like a sign language talk.

He was either going to eat me, or kill me, or both. I was sure of it. My thoughts raced and I started rushing, speeding up my pace so he wouldn't reach me. The faster I walked, the faster he walked, and he continued signaling to me as I looked back under my armpits. He was faster than me, and I was starting to feel exhausted. When he was a couple of feet away from me, he finally asked, "Child, did you lose something?"

"Yes!" I replied feeling jumpy.

"What was it?" he inquired.

"I lost my school money. I am going to school at the Lycée of Gisanze and I lost my tuition money…" I was ready to give every detail of my life to this stranger if he were willing to listen and help me find my tuition money.

"Where did you put it?" he asked.

"I wrapped it in a small white handkerchief, and —" I wanted to volunteer the rest of the details, but he interrupted me to ask, "Did it look like this?" He showed me the little hanky.

"Yes." I said with a trembling voice, longing for a good emotional release, but I was afraid the stranger might notice how scared I was, decide to eat me instead, and take my money after all. So, I decided to sound grown up. He handed me the handkerchief still wrapped. I didn't even open it to see whether indeed my money was still there or to count it. I was just grateful my hanky was still wrapped and white.

"Thank you, thank you, and thank you so very much!" I said to him. Before he left to continue his day, I braced myself and mumbled, "I would like to give you some of the money to thank you, but it is for the school tuition…" (Great, now I sounded too cheap). Although I itched with guilt for not giving him a monetary reward, there was no way for me to do so without falling short on the tuition.

"No child, you don't need to give me anything, just rush and get to school before sunset," he said and left. Aha, the sunset! That woke me up from my dream because it felt so surreal that some-one was being so kind toward a vulnerable kid in the middle of nowhere. I thanked him again, but I felt that my words were not enough to express my gratitude. He went on his way. I am sure God has blessed him for me, and I am thankful.

When I arrived at school, the classes had already been dismissed. I met some girls walking around the school neighborhood, taking in the evening breeze. The wind was quiet, the sky blue, and no one knew what I had gone through that day. I had missed my first day of school, but I had gained so much more on this journey—the confidence of bringing myself to school under God's watchful eye.

After Uncle Vincent heard about the ordeal I'd gone through, he decided that for Easter break, I would not go home. He sent me the fare to go to Bujumbura only and spend the two weeks of Easter vacation at my dad's second cousin's house. I wasn't happy about not seeing my parents and siblings during the Easter holidays, and not being checked out to see whether I had grown another quarter of an inch, but two weeks in the big city of Bujumbura were better than the bike ride to the pastor's house. Not that I didn't appreciate his kindness, but there were no kids to play with at his house. He lived with another evangelist, and I had no one to talk to. They went preaching most of the day, and prayed almost all night long. So, I truly thank Ananias, he was there for me at one of the impor-tant events in my youth more than my own father.

After that first year in high school, Uncle Vincent arranged to transfer me to another high school nearer to home, but far enough that it took me two days to walk there. There wasn't any high school in my province of Makamba at that time, let alone in my home-town. I was relieved, but also disappointed by the transfer. I would not see again all the friends I had made in seventh grade. In addi-tion, even though it was an ordeal to go to the Lycée of Gisanze, at least I had taken transportation—something on wheels. But at the new school, I would be walking my butt off each and every time I would go to school or come home. It was a very exhausting trip, all on foot.

CHAPTER 7 EVOLVING QUESTIONS FOR REFLECTION

1. Whenever I tell my childhood tales to my children, they are amazed of the ordeal of my going to school, which is very different from their experiences. What was high school like for you?

_____

_____

_____

_____

_____

2. What lessons did you learn from your high school years that you could pass on to others?

_____

_____

_____

_____

_____

3. Who can you share those lessons with?

_____

_____

_____

_____

_____

Chapter 8

ATTENDING A NEW SCHOOL

I am climbing a difficult road; but the glory gives me strength.
—Sextus Propertius

I started eighth grade at the Lycée of Rubanga, a high school located in the province of Bururi (South of Burundi), in the township of Matana. I had to travel with a couple of other less than fortunate students who walked to high school, including Mathilda, who was in tenth grade and lived across the valley from our house. As soon as my mother learned about my transfer, she appointed Mathilda to look out for me as a kind of big sister when we walked to school. Whenever school began again, Mathilda and I would leave two days early in order to make it there on time. On my departure day, my oldest sister, Eugenie, woke me up at four in the morning, after she had packed my lunch and readied my breakfast. My mother would rush me, telling me to eat breakfast fast, but I couldn't eat that early. After she had irritated me enough with her nagging, I just gave up eating breakfast altogether. I wished I could go back to sleep, but I had to go to school.

My mother always accompanied me to Mathilda's house to make sure I wouldn't be alone on the journey to school. I remember that one time we got to Mathilda's house after she had left. Mother almost had a heart attack, she was so distressed. She accompanied me a couple of more miles to make sure I could catch up with Mathilda. I was more worried about my mother having to walk all the way back home alone. Fortunately, Mathilda had stopped and waited up for me. The first day of our journey, we set out in the early morning and walked past the big Mount Inanzegwe, a mountain of 7064 feet elevation. Not only was Mount Inanzegwe a high mountain to climb, but its rocks and cumbersome stones made it hard to walk. I was always beyond exhaustion when we finally arrived at the peak, only to realize that descending was as hard as climbing. People in the western world climb mountains for fun, as an adventure. For me, climbing Mount Inanzegwe was the only way to go to school.

At sunset, we went to spend the night at people's houses— people we didn't even know. We would just go to someone's house and say, "Hello, anybody home? We are students going to the Lycée of Rubanga, and we need a place to spend the night." Mathilda usually did the talking. I never saw any family refuse to house us for the night in my entire six years of going to that school. People were always very kind and understanding. They treated us for the night as special guests. After a while, we spotted a good family who would feed us well—a mix of rice and beans with palm butter—so we would stick with that family. Every new school year and during the holidays, the family would kind of expect us. And it wasn't only Mathilda and me. After we had walked several miles, we met with other students of various grades. Together, we went to spend the night with our favorite host. Unlike my former school, the Lycée of Rubanga was a gender mixed school, so there were boys and girls.

After we had joined the others, I enjoyed having older students help me to carry my luggage and walk at my slow pace when I was tired and sweating salt. I couldn't wait to have some place to sleep for the night, and I would sleep like a rock without moving any part of my little body. The next morning, which always came fast, we had to get up as early as possible since it would be our arrival day to school. I usually couldn't walk. My feet were so swollen that I had to limp. However, after a couple of miles walking, I had no other choice than to press on my feet to carry me to school. The second day was a little better than the first. There was no more mini-Everest to climb, only small hills and valleys, and usually a pleasant landscape to look at. Depending on how fast we were, the final leg of this trip usually took us between seven and eight hours.

Again, why all this going to school when it was so painful? By then, my parents had warmed up to the idea that I had to continue school. They had seen no potential in my farming skills, and they had decided that maybe, just maybe, one day I would marry someone important or be a government minister after all (president was out of the question). I could see my mother was determined that I would go to school no matter what. She saved up a little money from selling grains from our crops that she tended to so carefully at the market in the summer. She gave my brothers and me some money to buy school supplies such as notebooks, toiletries, and other little things we needed for school, so that Uncle Vincent only needed to give us the tuition money.

When we finally got to school, we were excited to see the other students, especially our friends, and hear all they had to say about what had happened over the vacation. But I was too tired to enjoy the reunion because my feet would be swollen for the entire week. Sometimes, Mathilda came to my dorm to see how I was doing and massaged my feet with hot water she got from the school kitchen. She took care of me just like my mother had asked her to do. After the first week, I felt better. I liked school; I liked learning, but not studying. My strengths were in literature and social studies, but these seemed to be my least favorite subjects. So, I didn't study much, getting by with only what the teacher had taught in the classroom. But I took math and the sciences seriously. Because my brother Cyriaque was a nerd in math and the sciences, I wanted to show him that I, too, a girl, could do well in those subjects. Physics and chemistry were very tough classes, but as I grew older, I got decent grades, although never high enough to guarantee me a placement in a scientific major.

After tenth grade, we had to be placed in senior high (grades 11 to 13), according to what we wanted to be when we grew up. Those who were strong in math and the sciences, were placed in the scientific majors—the future Einsteins! Cyriaque was one of those, but at a separate lycée, thank God! The idea of attending the same high school with my brother would have been terrifying. He was so book smart and too serious to enjoy the teenage life. I didn't want him yelling at me if I didn't get good grades in math or the sciences. But there was an unspoken responsibility on his part toward me; he wanted me to excel in those subjects, so I would wind up in a scientific major and follow in his footsteps. Soft subjects such as literature or social studies were kind of undervalued in Burundi.

I wasn't that bad in math, but I wasn't as nerdy as my brother. Even then, it was thought girls would be better off with social skills because they were expected to marry someone important; they wouldn't really need math skills or big degrees. As long as girls knew how to count money, supervise good housekeeping, and entertain social gatherings, they would be fine. There was also the stereotype that if a woman were too smart, men would be intimidated, which would make it hard to find a husband. So, educating a girl was like a business trying to increase its shareholders' value. The father could then expect two cows instead of one for his daughter's dowry, if she were educated just enough, but not too much. Thus, high school diplomas qualified women to get married to high ranking politicians, military officers, and even uneducated millionaires. Although one of my main objectives in going to school was to find an educated husband, I had a little voice in my head telling me not to settle for the cooking and the cleaning. By all means, I wanted to avoid having to live my mother's life. I wanted to be able to have choices my mom never had. Therefore, it was a good fortune that my innate knowledge in literature and languages afforded me the opportunity to continue in the upper grades that would qualify me to go to a university. That meant I needed to focus more on social studies, such as world history and geography, as well as more French literature and a little English.

After tenth grade, my placement in the literature major was in part due to my French literature teacher, Mr. Bokongo-Kasongo Freddy (from former Zaire). He was adamant that I would study literature and then go on to the university. I had actually decided that after tenth grade, I wanted to study nursing. I wanted to attend nursing school because it was well known for its good food. The students who went there reported being well-fed and well-tended. The Lycée of Rubanga fed us so poorly that I was often sick. I had decided that after tenth grade, I would go to nursing school so I would be well fed and maybe grow another couple of inches taller.

However, because I was part of the school's theatrical team, Mr. Bokongo refused to let me go to the nursing high school for my senior years. After tenth grade, the school-teacher committee had a say in recommending the placement of its students. Because of my involvement in the school plays, Mr. Bokongo wanted to keep me at the school for my upper grades. By staying at the Lycée of Rubanga, I was guaranteed to go to the university, if I passed the national exam, of course. I always played the lead role in the school plays, which had become popular. Mr. Bokongo was the head of the school's theatrical productions, which he chose and directed. We used to take our school plays on tour (just like Broadway!) to the other schools in the province and make good money for the school. Mr. Bokongo saw some potential in me, which I didn't know I had. I had a good French accent, so Mr. Bokongo always chose me for the lead female character in every single play. I loved it! Finally, someone was paying attention to me and believing in me. In addition, I had a good memory, so my brain would remember my lines the first time I read the script.

You see, I could have been a star if I'd had all the opportunities of an American girl and lacked all the obstacles of an African girl (no grudge here). My acting career resulted from my studying both French and African literature. I liked being on stage during plays. It was both scary and exhilarating, especially if the plays were good enough to provoke emotions. My character was always somehow good, always a person of integrity, and of course, I was some fairy princess facing cultural conflicts between modern and old times, new and old generations, especially in African literature. It was a treat.

I liked African authors because they wrote about stories their countries had lived, such as the Negro trade that ultimately became slavery in the U.S., or the colonialism and the post-colonial era. They also wrote about conflicts between generations, young versus old, urban versus village. Our school plays attracted the local community, intellectuals around the township of Matana, and especially, teachers and students from the Lycée of Matana, a boys only high school. They came to watch our plays on Saturday nights in the big refectory that we converted into a theatre with mounted tables and chairs and surrounded with huge drapes hanging from the ceiling. If you didn't know better, you would think it was a real stage. That refectory was a multipurpose room. We used it as a dining hall, of course; then on Saturdays after dinner, we transformed it into a dancing hall, and when we had plays, it became a theatre. My senior high school years went by pretty fast because I was having fun being in school. Although I was a shy girl, when on stage, I just lived in the moment and forgot all about my timidity. I thank Mr. Bokongo for the gift of validation.

In my entire thirteen years of high school education, there wasn't a time when I relaxed about the school tuition. I always had the same anxiety that my brothers and I would not have money and might miss the year. I was also feeling guilty about how we imposed on Uncle Vincent to pay for our schooling. Sometimes, we didn't receive the money until only two days before school was due to begin. And we didn't have paid summer work that could have helped us to earn money. The system was that there were no student paid jobs; we only worked for our families. We would have worked our butts off if there were such opportunities. Although Uncle Vincent always paid our tuition, and my father had come to rely on his brother's kindness, my brothers and I viewed it as imposing on our uncle and even begging. We were always mad at our father for never providing for our schooling needs.

There was one time Uncle Vincent had not sent us the money. My brother Cyriaque was attending the Lycée of Bururi, Emmanuel was in a technical high school in the province of Ngozi, and I was at the Lycée of Rubanga. We had been waiting for our uncle to send us the tuition money, but we still didn't have it two days before our schools were due to begin. We didn't know what to do. So, my brothers and I packed our bags and went to see Uncle Vincent where he worked. He was a colonel at a military base in the province of Bururi. We walked from home to where he lived for more than ten hours, but I loved it for once. It made me closer to my two older brothers. I felt the tuition issue was our shared struggle, and we made an unspoken pact that we had to succeed in school. We were the chosen ones, the lucky ones to attend high school, when so many of our age couldn't get past sixth grade. Often, neighbors scolded their children to make them succeed in school, referring to us as role model students in our village. There was this one neighbor whose father always told him, "Look at Gaspard's kids; why can't you be like them? What do they have that you don't?" As a matter of fact, most of the students who failed in school had fathers who could afford to pay for their tuition and were supportive.

When we arrived at Uncle Vincent's house, he wasn't expecting us, but he welcomed us anyway. Even though I am sure he instantly knew the motive of our visit, he asked us, "Why are you here? Shouldn't you be going to your respective schools?"

"We don't have tuition money," Cyriaque took the lead and answered. I could hear his voice shaking in anger (as if to say, "Why would you even ask that question Uncle?")

"Who am I? Your father? Shouldn't you discuss tuition money with your father?" Uncle Vincent let us have it for once, but he was too kind to mean it.

"Our father always says he has no money for our tuition, and he cannot afford to send us to high school." Again poor Cyriaque answered for all of us. Emmanuel just opened his big eyes and said nothing. And I kept quiet, not knowing how we would pull it off this time. Uncle Vincent was only telling us that he was starting to get tired of our financial dependency on him, but he had no way out. My father felt entitled to his younger brother's money. It was how the system worked, and still works today. Those in families who are well off have to pay the price. Everyone understands that and comes to expect it.

My uncle was paying our tuition as a service to his extended family. He knew that if we did well in school and graduated, we would be the next good Samaritans for our other relatives. What I loved about my uncle was that he didn't just give us money for tuition and then forget about us. He expected us to do well in school. He had said time and again, "If you fail a grade, and have to repeat it, don't count on me to pay twice for the same grade." As a matter of fact, if we boasted that we had ranked second place in a trimester, he would ask us, "What prevented you from being the first in your class?" and he expected it the next term. My brothers and I did well in high school. However, Emmanuel didn't pass the national exam, which short-cut his education so he couldn't continue to university. But at least he finished high school with a technical diploma in agriculture. I was glad someone demanded hard work from me in school. To my father, school was just a way to escape home chores, but to Uncle Vincent, we were in school for a noble purpose. He was the pioneer of education in our family.

It was finally a relief for Uncle Vincent when I entered my last year of high school. Cyriaque had graduated two years before and entered the military academy. With his technical diploma, Emmanuel entered the work force. Uncle Vincent could finally relax; he got married the year before I graduated from high school. His military career was steady and rewarding. He was the first to be honored with the ranking of General in the country, and he later became Burundi's minister of defense. In 2009, he was sent to New York as a military attaché, representing Burundi to the United Nations, which was his last position before he retired at sixty years old in 2013.

The last year of high school, we had to pass another national exam that helped determine who could go to the university. I got the required passing score, but no scholarship that would allow me to study abroad. After grade thirteen, it was every student's dream to get a scholarship to study abroad. But only a few select students did. If your grade point average was extra high, some scholarships were available from some Western organizations or countries as part of the international aid to Burundi. Many were from our previous colonizer, Belgium. Other scholarships were from China, the Soviet Union, and other European countries. Several other coveted foreign aid scholarships existed, but you had to be the son or daughter of an influential person in the country to get one, or your parents needed to pay a fat bribe. Even being a nerd didn't guarantee a scholarship abroad. In some exceptions, if a nerd got it, he was sent to the less than "attractive" countries. Only a few elite kids got what they wanted and were sent to the Western nations, which were far more attractive to young high school graduates because where you studied determined the career opportunities you would have once you returned to Burundi.

In the summer of 1987, I graduated from high school, praise the Lord! A week later, Cyriaque took his first flight to France. He had passed the test that qualified him for a scholarship abroad, and he was sent to a university in Aix-en-Provence, France. I cried for joy when I accompanied my brother to the airport. I was so proud of him. He encouraged me, told me to study economics at the university, and not to fool with boys. He was overprotective of me and didn't want any boy fooling around with me. He never wanted me near men, especially military officers. He used to tell me that our family had enough military people (which was true—many of my cousins who had failed sixth grade were in the barracks). He would tell me that if I married (when he would let me), it had to be someone outside the army. I understood the constant danger of people in the army, so I took Cyriaque's words seriously.

After Cyriaque left for France, I took the bus home to my parents to report on my graduation and my brother's leaving. Dad wasn't impressed, but he knew there was no going back. There was no graduation party for me, and I didn't really expect it. However, I longed for a little praise from my father. Since I had passed the national test that qualified me for university admission, I knew better days were ahead of me, and I was so ready for my wonder years to begin.

CHAPTER 8 EVOLVING QUESTIONS FOR REFLECTION

1. Were there any obstacles for you when you were attending high school?

_____

_____

_____

_____

_____

2. If so, what were they?

_____

_____

_____

_____

_____

3. Who was involved in helping you overcome them?

_____

_____

_____

_____

_____

Chapter 9

REMINISCING ABOUT MY UNIVERSITY YEARS

The true sign of intelligence is not knowledge but imagination.
—Albert Einstein

In the fall of 1987, I was a university freshman. The vast majority of high school graduates who had passed the national exam entered the one and only university in the country—the University of Burundi. I wasn't going to whine about not studying abroad because I had achieved beyond my wildest expectations.

I had been placed in arts and humanities despite my dislike of these two fields; the ministry of education had disregarded my choice to attend the school of journalism. Journalism was my first choice because I wanted to be a French TV news anchor. I was always mesmerized by journalists who read news in French on the television. With my good pronunciation, I was certain I could be just like them. However, the ministry of education enrolled me in arts and humanities instead, even though it was my third choice. Had I been a math nerd, I would have studied economics like my brother Cyriaque had asked me to. In Burundi, economics was and is still highly regarded as a field of study that helps one to be considered for high paying jobs. Economists used to find good jobs in banks and the government, and they were more eligible for international organizations such as the World Bank or the International Monetary Fund. Arts and humanities mostly guaranteed a teaching job, most likely in a remote area for the rest of my life. Teaching in Burundi is the most underpaid and under-promoted job. With such a degree, opportunities don't knock on one's door.

My high school trauma being over, I now had a shot at a better life. At the university, I would start wearing real shoes, not just the click-clack flip flops I had all high school long. No problem— I could afford shoes and clothes because in addition to housing the students and feeding them for free, the University of Burundi gave us an allowance. Each month, those who lived on campus got around 3,000 Burundi francs (roughly three U.S. dollars today) but at that time, it was worth much more than it is nowadays. And those who chose to live outside the campus received even more money in allowance. I had no other bills to pay, so each month, I sent some money to my mother, and once in a-while, I sent money to my two younger siblings, Thérèse and Francis who were still in high school. I was rich!

The first couple of months at the University of Burundi were torturous if you were a spoiled brat, and my family had awarded me that title long ago. The first weeks, all freshmen had to go through an initiation ritual performed mostly by the sophomores, because they were doing what had been done to them the previous year, when they were freshmen themselves. They started their session of initiation early in the month of September, when it was time for registration at the main campus located in the capital city.

I remember my first initiation when I went to register. I was staying again at dad's second cousin where I had spent my Easter holiday in seventh grade. He seemed to be the only relative living in the capital at that time. On registration day, I walked to the registrar's office from his house, only three miles away. I had been told that on registration days, I would encounter the *"poil"* (pronounced: pwal, and meaning "the initiated"). You could only be called a *"poil"* if you had gone through the initiation, called *"baptême"* (baptism") as if you were "born-again". I don't recall my captor's name, but I remember being approached by a young man (it seemed boys enjoyed doing this initiation to girls). He asked me a couple of smart questions that were typically asked of the *"puants"* (those enduring the initiation rites and literally meaning "stinky"). That's right, freshmen smelled bad! The *"poils"* called themselves, "the omnipotent, omnipresent, and omniscient," just like God! They said we *"puants"* had some type of bug they needed to get out of our systems. We were also called "blue," another term used to describe our naiveté.

Coming from all over the country to the university, most freshmen didn't know what they were stepping into. Really even here in America, when they start college or university, how many kids know what they are stepping into? Even some parents are freaked out when their kids go to college. Not that my parents were freaked out by my going to the university. By then, they had admitted my potential to be somebody myself, and not just marry somebody.

After answering the smart questions my initiator asked me, I was released to go and register, but he promised me that he would still be there when I returned from the registrar's office. I panicked; I anticipated humiliation on the Boulevard du 28 Novembre, a road located a couple of feet from the university, where the *poils* waited for freshmen to introduce them to the initiation rites during the registration period. At that U-turn road, the traffic was very busy, and it was a treat for passersby to enjoy some humor in the initiation scene. But it was the worst nightmare for us, the "stinky." It was even worse if somebody who knew you saw you being humiliated on the streets. Fortunately, in my entire initiation time, no one outside the university community ever saw me performing the rituals. I survived that first day of initiation because when I came out of the registrar's office, all the *poils* had gone to lunch, and I went home as fast as I could before they came back. But the initiation was only postponed until university classes began.

When classes started, the initiations were only performed during recess, or during lunch and dinner times. That's when our inner strengths were put to the test. If you weren't up to the torture of being initiated, you couldn't eat, and even if you ate, it was with such anxiety! Some girls just gave up going to the dining hall altogether and cooked on their portable stoves in their campus rooms. Others who had relatives nearby went to their houses for meals. I didn't have a close relative nearby with whom I felt comfortable enough to go to for meals. Even if I had, I wouldn't want to impose or take advantage of my relative just because I was afraid of being "baptized." So, I made up my mind that whatever torture there would be, I would endure it. This was a very smart move on my part because the more I did whatever the rituals of the day were, the more I got the hang of it, and the less I was anguished by the whole initiation process.

The rituals were nothing traumatic if you were brave enough. Mostly, the *poils* wanted us to sing loudly lyrics containing names of female and male private parts. We had to perform those lyrics in front of other students and anyone who happened to pass by. In addition, girls were asked to grab, lift up, and hold tightly our breasts that the *poils* called "stones." And freshmen boys were asked to grab, lift up, and hold tightly onto their balls. And in unison, we would declaim in French, "*J'empoigne mes pierres!*" ("I'm grabbing my stones!") Saying the private body parts in French was somehow bearable, but if asked to say them in Kirundi, and come up with ten synonyms for each private part was the most humiliating thing. I'd just whisper the words with shyness in my voice, and then my initiator would say, "Repeat more loudly, Stinky, so every *poil* can hear you." I would then repeat just as softly, only to make my initiator more upset, and be ordered to repeat it ten times louder, under the cackling laughs of those watching. After saying those words time and again, I felt dirty and truly needed a shower! When my initiator was satisfied that I had been humiliated enough, he would set me free to go and eat. I was always caught when going to the dining hall. I had to eat, you know.

The next day, the *poils* would see me again and make sure I endured the same as the day before. Depending on the special initiation menu of the day, I would do whatever they asked to get my meal. After a couple of days seeing me coming and going, the *poils* laughed at me. I remember one guy saying, "*Puante*, you're back? Why aren't you frightened like the other girls and go eat at Auntie's house? Huh? Oh, wait! You have no auntie in the city?" He would then rub his beard he had grown for the occasion. That hurt my feelings because I actually wished I had an auntie in the city, some immediate family I could count on to hide me during the initiation period. But my immediate family lived in my hometown, and I only had distant relatives in the capital city. I had to be strong and pass this initiation if I wanted to stay in school.

I had come a long way, and no initiation would have stopped me from getting an education. I continued to go through the "baptism" and get my three meals a day at the dining hall. After a week or so, I had the nicknames "Daring Freshman" and "Brave *Puante*" because I didn't chicken out during the initiation time. That earned me respect from the *poils* and the admiration of the *puants* —the stinky! Some of my peers would ask me, "Seconde, how do you do it? How come you're not afraid of the *poils*?"

"I need my three meals, girlfriend!" I would tell my freshmen mates. In less than two weeks, the *poils* had stopped harassing me, and I was set free. If an unknowing *poil* tried to stop me, I would hear another one say, "Let her go."

Those who had been trying to hide in order to avoid the initiation were severely punished if they were apprehended. They were dipped in a muddy ditch the *poils* called *Muchuti River*, which served as a drain, located in front of the main campus restaurant. This, for girls, was the ultimate death sentence since they didn't want to mess up their clothes or make-up. I was never dipped in the *Muchuti River*. Only reluctant (recalcitrant) *puants*, those who refused to obey the rules of the initiation, were dumped in that ditch.

The initiation's wrap-up day was on a Saturday, close to a month after the academic year had started. That's when classes started heating up and professors started getting in the mood for serious teaching after three months of vacation. On Saturday afternoon, all the important *poils* lined up all the stinky freshmen. I couldn't contain my amusement at the *poils'* self-importance, —some even wore ties to mark the closing ceremonies. We were ordered to march from the main campus of Mutanga to Ngangara, another campus approximately three miles away, to meet up with the freshmen from other campuses. When we arrived at the other campus, we were set free. We became *poils* ourselves and were allowed to socialize with the other students. It felt like a graduation from "Stinky High" for me; it was a coming of age in its own right. We would be the ones performing the same rituals the following year to the freshmen to keep the tradition alive. I never baptized anybody in my entire academic life. Although it was a delight to watch when it was being done to others, I wasn't able to torture another soul. (I know, sweet me.) Despite its unpleasantness, I think the initiation was needed.

It was a rite of passage from high school to university. It opened my eyes and made me a little stronger in facing the academic life.

The first year at my campus dorm, I shared a room with another girl who was studying economics. The room was big enough for both of us. Personally, I didn't have a lot of stuff, so it was more than large enough. My roommate was a very beautiful girl, but very shy. Men, ranging from university students to professionals, tried so hard to get her to go on a date with them, but she always turned them down. That first year, classes were a bit challenging for me because I wasn't used to the academic way of studying. Taking notes while professors lectured was an art in itself. I failed two classes and had to retake exams for them in September, fortunately passing that time.

My second year, the university finished a new building and all the sophomores were the lucky ones to move into the new rooms. The rooms had been built with some extra nice features, such as a bathroom inside each room, instead of the shared bathrooms we had the previous year. There was a sink and a mirror above the sink—really cool. We also shared rooms. Roommates were assigned by the university's logistic affairs office. My roommate and I didn't exactly become BFFs. From the beginning, she built a wall between us that could be read as, "Stay away from me; I'll stay away from you." And it stayed that way for the entire year. She and I weren't of the same ethnic background, which seemed to be the problem. Old wounds between Tutsis and Hutus had been reopened in 1988, when killings occurred in the Northern provinces, especially in Muyinga (where I had spent my seventh grade year); as a result, university students were very apprehensive about their ethnic belonging.

No doubt, my roommate and I were playing ethnicity politics without any spoken words. Our non-verbal language said it all.

Because she was a Hutu and I, a Tutsi, we just chose to stay away from each other, only talking when absolutely necessary, such as to clarify what was for lunch for that day or to complain about it. However, in my heart of hearts, I believed my roommate would never hurt me, and I think she had the same trust in me.

My roommate was studying the sciences, and I was studying arts and humanities. Again this made for a difficult match. Scientific students kind of looked down on people of literary endeavors as if we had nothing to learn, nothing new at least. In the science majors, students studied nonstop. We used to joke that they didn't seem to feel the mosquito bites, while we, the students of literature, we had boys coming into our rooms to kill the mosquitoes for us. I remember one time a male student came into my room, and after a long silence (because he was too shy to ask me out), he started swatting mosquitoes. He got this poor mosquito into his hand and gallantly crushed it, showing off how heroic he could be. I imagined him saying, "You see, girl if you go out with me, I will take care of you. I will kill all the mosquitoes in the Bujumbura valley; I will kill all the mosquitoes in the whole tropical world." Students in science studied as if there were no tomorrow, while in literature, we enjoyed life on the campus, discovering, you know—each other on a deeper level.

But it was my roommate who had a boyfriend, a serious one, and not me! They were actually engaged. Whenever her man came to see her in the room we shared, I would get out of the room, not because they forced me to, but because I knew when two consenting adults needed their privacy. I never failed to give her space when her boyfriend visited her in our room. I would go into my best friend Beatrice's room instead, to catch up on the gossip. Beatrice and I were best friends since our second year at the university. Whenever her roommate wasn't in the room, I would sneak in and we'd talk and giggle, then count our miseries of not having boyfriends. After, we would enjoy music on her radio and sing our hearts out to Paul Young's "Every time you go away, you take a piece of me with you…."

Prime and Freddy were my male best friends since high school and at the university. They offered me a brotherly friendship devoid of sexual intentions. And I appreciated them for that. When we were in high school, most boys were drawn to girls only to experience sex. In some cases, that resulted in a teen pregnancy that ended a girl's education in the blink of an eye. Whenever my kids ask me whether I had a boyfriend before meeting their dad, I tell them that I only had guy friends, not boyfriends.

My dating act started right on track in my junior year, with a man who was sent by relatives who meant well. And he was a working adult. Because I viewed dating students as a pastime, I played a little hard to get. Given that I was a late bloomer, I didn't want to waste my time with a boy who wasn't a "somebody" yet. I needed a short-cut in life for once. I wanted a man who would make me his wife. Many girls in the junior and senior years were married, others engaged, and others like me were starting to venture out into the dating arena. My well meaning relatives were really looking out for the right match for me. It seemed as if one relative wanted me to marry one man, while others absolutely, definitely refused to hear about him. Therefore, I was confused. I asked myself, "Do I have a say in whom I marry?" Sometimes in the Burundian culture, it's not clear who decides. Because for our parents, marriages were an arranged business, relatives and friends had a big say in the man a girl would marry. Those traditions more or less still apply today. Your family members don't force you to marry someone anymore, but they definitely have a say or want to have a say. I dated three men before meeting the one I married.

One afternoon, near the end of my junior year, a man called Claver arrived at my dorm as a message carrier. Ironically, he was just passing by to deliver a letter to a girl on campus, and that girl happened to be me. He was working at the University of Burundi as an Assistant Professor in the faculty of Applied Sciences. He had started that job a couple of months after he had returned from China where he had spent five years studying for his Engineering degree.

So Claver came on the campus where I stayed, to deliver the letter Uncle Vincent had sent me from Russia, where he was on a mission for work. He had given that letter to one of his colleagues who happened to be Claver's cousin, and who had just returned from Russia. So Claver came with his sister to bring me my letter; his sister was on the same campus I was and knew me. After I opened and read the letter, we chatted a little bit. I could see that he had something he wanted to say, but he was too embarrassed to say it. After a seemingly agonizing moment, he gathered his courage and said, "Can we go out and drink tea?"

I said, "No thank you, I don't drink tea."

Then he said, "Do you drink water? We can drink water."

I looked at him and thought to myself, "Really, you want to take me out and give me water?" but instead, I told him I had things to do. He was disappointed, but he promised me he would be back. And he came back! I gave him a hard time again until he gave up. Only later would our lives be brought together unexpectedly, and we would start dating. It seemed as if the universe were playing some kind of trick on me because, although my uncle loved me, he had never written to me before, and now because of his letter, I had found a man!

Once we had been dating for a couple of months, Claver and I were both certain we had found the "one" in each other—we had no doubt about it. We knew we would get married, but we were nowhere near being ready. Then, I found out I was pregnant before I could finish spelling m-o-t-h-e-r-h-o-o-d. I certainly didn't get a chance to ask for a definition or put it into a sentence. My pregnancy automatically set our premature wedding engagement, but we hadn't taken time to know each other, to talk about having babies or discuss our future life together. Furthermore, we had no money. Claver's job wasn't paying him enough to support the three of us once the baby would come, and I was still in school. When I was exactly eight months pregnant, in June of 1991, we had our wedding. We were so broke that we couldn't even afford a wedding cake, so we settled for fruit cups instead. I don't know who came up with this idea of fruit cups, but it worked! No honeymoon either, because the following Monday, I was back in class to take my finals and finish my degree.

CHAPTER 9 EVOLVING QUESTIONS FOR REFLECTION

1. Was attending a college or university part of your education?

_____

_____

_____

_____

_____

2. If so, how was your experience, and what did it teach you about life?

_____

_____

_____

_____

_____

3. Who in your life are you most grateful to for helping you achieve your education?

_____

_____

_____

_____

_____

Chapter 10
BECOMING A
FIRST TIME MOTHER

Motherhood has a very humanizing effect.
Everything gets reduced to essentials.
— Meryl Streep

After our wedding, Claver and I rented one bedroom in a house we shared with three bachelors. Two of them were my husband's best friends. Since learning that I was pregnant, these friends had decided that the baby I was carrying would be, without fail, a pretty baby. So, they had a name for her before she was born. They called my baby "Jolie" (which means "pretty" in French), and they called me "Mama Jolie." The name felt so real and so beautiful that I was proud my womb was carrying such a pretty baby. I was in my last year of university then. It wasn't a small feat doing school-work while being pregnant, but I passed my finals with flying colors. I had finished the demographic research I needed to write my thesis, so all I had left to do was write it, and my topic and outline were ready to roll. Therefore, after my final exams in June 1991, I only had to focus on the baby. Our baby Jolie came into the world in July of 1991, a month after our wedding. As the two friends had predicted, baby Jolie (we later called her Carmelle) was really pretty. She was chubby, with pink cheeks, and big eyes, and yes, great lips! She was born a month before my husband was to leave for Canada for his graduate studies. I was very happy for him, and I tried to file in the back of my mind my worries of staying alone with the baby.

Within a week of the delivery, although I felt the joy of being a new mommy and I was surrounded by family and friends, I felt an uneasiness I didn't quite know how to explain. I didn't eat as well as I should have after having a baby. I didn't have an appetite. I found too many people to be overwhelming, too noisy, and too exhausting. You know when you feel sick, but you cannot identify with clarity what the problem is? But I had to be strong and put on a smile for all the guests who came to congratulate us on our new-born. I felt moody, and I would hide and cry. At night, I had to wake up to breastfeed, and I didn't catch up on sleep during the day. The heat and humidity of Bujumbura doubly affected me. And besides my emotional pain, I still had physical pains and dis-comforts from the long labor during the delivery (it had taken nine hours from the first contraction to final delivery). My sutures down there on the tear had come off before it was completely healed, so they had to be redone. I had anesthesia, but I felt the whole thing being stitched back together anyway.

As if all that weren't enough, my husband was not available to be with me. He had his work, and after work, there were many people who needed him for their personal projects. How did I react to that? I cried, of course. Furthermore, his scholarship to go to Canada came, so he would be gone the month following my deliv-ery. All those emotions just kept filling me with pain, but I didn't complain. To be honest, I didn't know if I had a right to complain or if there was anything to complain about. After all, my life was in full bloom. I had everything I had ever wanted—a handsome husband (if only he could be more available and spend more time with me) and a baby (without any major complications other than the tear). But my breast milk wasn't filling up my breasts as it should, and I felt guilty about it. I was told by more experienced mothers to eat more food and to drink more in order to have abundant breast milk, but I just couldn't. And I hadn't gained any weight during pregnancy, so I was fairly skinny by the African standards of what a new mother should weigh. I felt guilty about that too because people kept asking me, "How come you didn't gain any weight? What's wrong with you?"

Eventually, my husband's day to leave arrived. He left me with this brand new baby and lots of help from both my and his sides of the family. So, really I wasn't alone, or so I tried to convince myself. It was only after his departure that I started feeling very heavy. I didn't cry when I said goodbye to him at the airport. Everybody was watching me to see my tears, but for the first time in my life, I hid my emotions. I wanted to show my husband that I was woman enough to handle the baby during his absence. I didn't cry because I was on too much of an emotional roller-coaster, and I wanted to conceal it from him and the others around me. But mostly, I didn't cry because I knew that if I started, I wouldn't be able to stop, and I was at the airport. My sister-in-law and my younger sister kept teasing me that I had to cry because my husband was leaving. It wasn't until we got back home that I couldn't contain it anymore. My heart just couldn't bear the heaviness; it felt as if someone had dropped twenty pounds on it slowly, without breaking the arteries, and managed to leave it there for the day. I exploded in tears. My two helpers then felt terrible, thinking it was their fault that I was crying because of their teasing. My crying had nothing to do with the two sisters. In fact, I was grateful that they were there for me.

My emotions had boiled up and were just too much to keep in. Then I looked at my feet, and my fingers, and realized that they looked suddenly swollen. As I took notice of this body change, I saw that after my long cry, my eyes and face were also swollen. All of a sudden, I was a little chubbier than usual. I thought that because I hadn't had swollen feet during my pregnancy, the swelling must come after birth for some women. I worried less about my physical change than I did about my emotional heaviness. My sister and my sister-in-law, my two new care-takers for the next year or so, worried about my swollen ankles and fingers. Even my wedding band, which had been loose before, started to fit perfectly. "Okay! Maybe this is the weight I am expected to gain after delivery," I reasoned with myself. "But what if I were sick with swollen ankles, fingers, and eyes; what could that be?" I tried to self-diagnose. The next day, I was swollen all over.

My sister Thérèse looked at me worryingly. "Don't look at me with those eyes; I am perfectly fine!" I yelled at her.

"I think you need to see a doctor," Thérèse said.

"A doctor? What for? I am perfectly fine. I don't feel any pain, besides my lack of appetite," I told her. By the third day of my swelling, however, both sisters and I agreed that it was better if I took the case to the doctors. The next day, I took a cab to *Roi-Khaled* Hospital, the country's medical school that housed an in and out-patient hospital as well. Roi- Khaled Hospital used to be Burundi's first decent hospital in the 1990s, but nowadays, it is in disarray. I showed the doctor my swollen everything and answered his questions. He was a doctor in residency in his last year of medical school, and he knew me from the university's dining hall. Some of the resident doctors in training had met me or even "baptized" me during my freshmen year.

The doctor's response worried me more than it comforted me. He told me I could have a very dangerous case of kidney failure that could equally damage my liver, lungs, pancreas, and who knows what other major organ? Ouch! He prescribed me some magic pills that were supposed to drain the excess fluids in my body. "We will see how it goes," were his final words that day. Warning! I was not allowed to breastfeed baby Jolie during this treatment because the medication could be dangerous to her. My stomach instantly tied into a knot. "So, I'm not allowed to breastfeed my Jolie? Are you crazy, Doc?" Of course I didn't say that to him; I just went home and wept.

I started the medication as soon as I got home, so I could get better fast and start breastfeeding my baby again. Now, she would have to be on a bottle for a couple of days, maybe two weeks, depending on how long the medication would take. Oh dear, I hated the bottle! I didn't trust that it was sanitized enough to give to my baby. I told the nanny to boil the bottles so much when washing them before giving milk to the baby that she was afraid of melting the nipples (the bottle nipples of course, not mine).

The first time I gave the bottle to baby Jolie, she refused to take it. She was six weeks old. I felt like a tyrant forcing her to drink bottled baby formula. It was the guiltiest moment of my life. How could I be sick when my baby needed me to feed her with the most nutritious milk in the world? And her daddy was far away on another continent. Not that he would have picked up the breastfeeding, but still, I wanted to face this with him! I felt like a total failure. I struggled with these feelings but I didn't share much with anybody. People around me just assumed I was handling it beautifully, given the circumstances. Even when my husband called me from Canada, I told him I was fine and everything was under control. I didn't want to burden him with my problems; he had graduate studies to finish. In addition, he was too far away to be of any help to me at that moment. I kept taking the medication, but when I was half-way done, one of my husband's relatives, who was a nurse, booked me to see a specialist.

Dr. Nzeyimana was a brilliant doctor who had specialized in internal medicine, and he was very well known in the medical community. I went to see him and explained what had happened. "I have a new baby," I said, "and because of the medication I'm not able to breastfeed," Then I burst out crying.

"I understand completely," Dr. Nzeyimana comforted me. "What kind of medication are you taking?"

When I told him what kind of medication I was on, he told me to stop taking it. Instead, he suggested that I work with him by taking urine samples every morning and bringing them to the hospital laboratory for analysis. So, every morning I would pee as much as I could. Some days, there wasn't enough urine because I was dehydrated from the medication I'd been taking. And I had been told not to drink too much water so I could reduce the fluids in my body. But I still managed to get a can of pee to bring to the hospital every day. The purpose of urine samples was for Dr. Nzeyimana to analyze how much protein my kidneys were filtering. Depending on the level of protein traces in my pee, he could tell whether or not my kidneys were performing to their full potential. "And let's not call this kidney failure please," Dr. Nzeyimana said. "I've seen worse and your case is nowhere near that." He even said I could resume breastfeeding.

"Halleluiah, thank you!" I said, almost bouncing off my seat in his office. I couldn't wait to get home to my baby Jolie.

I tried one breast, but baby Jolie didn't understand what the heck I was doing to her—harassing her with my breast in her mouth. After almost two weeks of no breastfeeding, my breasts were completely dried out. My nipples could have given her lips blisters if I had continued to force her. Baby Jolie had decided that since the bottle provided more milk flow, she wasn't going to settle for less. I cried, this time not openly. I had failed to breastfeed my baby, and now that I was ready, she was refusing it. I almost took it personally. Some women told me not to give her the formula, a proven strategy mothers use to deprive the baby until she is hungry and accepts the breast milk. I never tried that tip. I had already failed to breastfeed my first-born, so I just let her enjoy her baby formula. There was nothing else I could do. In the end, she was a healthy baby, apparently with no grudge over the lack of breast milk. I was the one who was hard on myself, as usual.

Dr. Nzeyimana continued my urine analysis and told me not to take salt or eat too much salty food. I settled for unsalted hard-boiled eggs to bring up my protein intake. The doctor never prescribed any medication again. Within a month, he told me I was cured. After that, I would only provide urine for checkups once a month.

I finished my formal thesis and presented it in front of a university jury in February 1992. In the meantime, I had been gathering traveling documents, and I had them ready at the beginning of March. I took my very first flight to Canada in March 1992 to join my husband. Just before I left to go to Canada, I went to ask Dr. Nzeyimana to give me some type of referral letter that explained what had happened to me, and what the doctors in Canada could do to help me if I ever had another problem. He congratulated me on going to Canada where medicine was far more advanced than in Burundi. He gave me a referral letter and wished me well. He said I'd had a minor case provoked by bacteria (I don't recall the medical term) that is usually fought by the immune system. But because of my post-delivery fragile condition, my immune system was too weak to kick in. Once in Canada, I went for regular checkups, and I have not had any related problems since. I thank the Lord for sustaining me during those hard postpartum times.

CHAPTER 10 EVOLVING QUESTIONS FOR REFLECTION

1. Parenthood is the most challenging job we'll ever do! But some parents are better at it than others. Take a moment and reflect on your own experiences as a parent.

_____

_____

_____

_____

_____

2. What do you wish you knew then that you know now? And if you're not a parent yet, what do you wish to learn about parenthood?

_____

_____

_____

_____

_____

3. What's the most important lesson you would pass on to your children or grandchildren in regards to being a parent?

_____

_____

_____

_____

_____

Part 2: North America

THE GROWN UP YEARS

Chapter 11

STARTING FROM SCRATCH

No matter how far a person can go, the horizon is still way beyond you.
—Zora Neale Hurston

Thanks to the government of Burundi's support to spouses of postgraduate students who were sent abroad, I was granted a plane ticket to go to Canada and join my husband. In March 1992, I came to Canada seven months after my husband had left Burundi. He was on a full scholarship from the Canadian International Development Agency. Burundi then paid for the families of students to reunite them with their spouses. The government of Burundi also gave us a family allowance, nothing much, but it was helpful. Combined with the allowance and what the scholarship paid toward my husband's living expenses, our monthly income was no more than $1,000 US. We lived in the province of Québec, in the city of Sherbrooke, an hour and half south of Montreal. Because the city was small and inexpensive, and our family was still small too, we could manage. The only big institution in the city was the University of Sherbrooke.

My trip to Canada was my first time on an airplane. I was very careful when I walked through the Brussels airport with Carmelle.

When I stepped onto the moving walkway, I was sure I would fall and I almost did with Carmelle tied on my back, my carry-on luggage in one hand, and my huge winter coat in the other. We spent the night in an airport hotel, but I was too tired to be awed by the hotel's beauty. The next morning, I woke up early to catch the airport shuttle to catch the flight to the Mirabel International Airport in Montreal.

For any new-comer to North America, the first thing that strikes you is the size of things. The roads were bigger than anywhere else. The size of food in restaurants, the cups, the cars, everything looked big. Even the seasons, especially Québec winters, were colder and longer to boot. At first, I was excited to see the snow. I had only envisioned what snow looks like from my physical geography class at the University of Burundi, taught by a smart professor whose nickname was Mahuba. Mahuba would tell us many tales about the Western world because he had travelled a lot. He had a Ph.D. in physical geography, and often took visiting professorships in western countries' universities. Therefore, the image I had of snow was essentially what Mahuba had taught us in class. Because I arrived in Canada in March, there weren't a lot of snowy days left that year, but I got to see the snow fall twice. However, the accumulated snow on the ground was unbelievable. The city of Sherbrooke was a beautiful green in summer, but it turned into Siberia in winter. I had never been exposed to so much cold in my life. The cold winter forced me to do what I had never done in Burundi: wear pants. In Burundi, I had never dared to wear them. Country girls, in my time at least, didn't wear pants. It was not considered proper. Pants were normal wear only for city girls, whom I used to envy sometimes; they could wear what they liked without being censored. But for a country girl like me, a girl from a village, pants would have been an affront to my family. Sometimes I wore them in my campus dorm room, just to get a feel for what it would be like, but never outside. Until I arrived in Canada, little did I know that pants were the most worn clothing in North America! Now that I was going to have to wear pants because of the weather, it took away all the sexiness of wearing pants that I had always anticipated. It became my survival outfit rather than my show-off-your booty outfit.

That first year in Québec was quite an adjustment. First, I had to learn about grocery shopping and food prices. When I went to buy groceries, I could not believe how expensive they were (especially since I kept converting each dollar into Burundi francs). Some fruits I had taken for granted all my life in Burundi became a luxury. For instance, little blackberries I used to eat fresh off the bushes when I used to herd cows, now cost a lot, and they weren't even as sweet as what I was used to. Avocados that were almost free in Burundi cost a fortune in Canada and weren't even that good. I had yet to learn to eat the apples that seemed to be the most abundant (I had never seen apples before). Every single food tasted different and not as good. Definitely, my taste-buds had to adjust to my new home.

Along with the food adjustment, I had to learn how to cook—I mean on a stove and everything. When I got married, we had a houseboy who cooked, did laundry, and cleaned. Before I got married, I didn't cook because I lived and ate at the university dining hall. And in high school, students didn't have to cook. We did all other chores, except cooking. At home, well, I cooked, but not the same way I would have to cook once in Canada. Step by step, I improved my cooking and started making edible food.

The language in Québec was another big adjustment. Québec French sounded strange and different from the French I had been taught in school. I struggled with comprehension for at least six months. Television programs were my best teachers. After struggling with my listening comprehension, I got it. I could finally understand the jokes I watched on CBC's comedy show: "*Juste pour rire* (Just for Laughs)." Once I could understand the jokes, it was a delight to listen to people talk. I never missed that show and was addicted to it every Friday night. At the end of the show was a green cartoon that announced: "*Maman...c'est fini!* ("Mommy, it's over!") I felt disappointed each time the cartoon appeared to end the show. It was the first time I watched someone make fun of politicians (especially the federal prime minister, Jean Chrétien) and get away with it. To me, it was a true advancement in democracy.

It was very tough for immigrants to be integrated even if you spoke French. The five years I lived in Québec were full of fun, though. Universities in Montreal and Québec City had an intelligentsia of Burundians who were earning their Ph.D.s in this or that. Very smart people! We quite enjoyed social gatherings, especially on New Year's Eve. On weekends, we took turns inviting other Burundian and Rwandan families who lived in Sherbrooke or friends from Montreal to visit us. So, it didn't feel lonely. We were all full of hopes that one day, we would return to Burundi with all the credentials we had accumulated and help our country develop. At least that was the aim of most students who received scholarships.

However, the civil war of 1993 that broke out in Burundi took all that hope away. Many of the Burundian families living in Canada at that time sought refuge there since they couldn't return home. We had to make a living and started spreading out all over the country to earn it. But the job market was not always friendly when you were an immigrant. There were many highly educated immigrants who were unemployed or underemployed, especially in the fields of medicine and law. You could hold all the degrees in the world, but your skills went mostly unused. Immigrant doctors resolved to taxi driving when they should be working in the emergency room, operating room, and other medical practices. People who used to be in commanding positions in their countries were depressed and had to resign themselves to non-gratifying jobs.

The year 1995 in Québec was also a tough time because the province was trying to secede from Canada and become an independent country. Many immigrants who had become Canadian citizens voted against the separation of Québec from Canada, as had many powerful money-makers, including big companies, banks, and the financial community in general. As I watched the news every day, I learned that some big Canadian companies were threatening to move their headquarters from Montreal to Toronto, Calgary, Vancouver, or other big financial centers. Some of the U.S. companies established in Québec also projected withdrawing their businesses from an independent Québec. Residents of other provinces were afraid that a separation of one of the biggest Canadian provinces would ignite a disintegration of the whole country, both demographically and economically. Immigrants were very anxious, and those who had settled would have to make a decision whether to leave Québec and start over in other provinces. The separation proposal —"*Le Non Québécois*" as it was famously referred to, narrowly lost with a rounded 49 percent of the population voting "Yes" for Québec to secede from Canada, and 51 percent against the motion to secede. Jacques Parizeau, Québec's premier who had initiated the referendum, was very disappointed. In his concession speech, he blamed the "money and the ethnic vote" for the defeat.

Nine months after I arrived in Canada, life started being much more routine. I was entertained by Camii (as we nicknamed our daughter Carmelle; we didn't keep Jolie), who was now a toddler and a Little Miss Sunshine in her terrific twos, but it wasn't what I had envisioned before I came. My husband was a full-time graduate student at the University of Sherbrooke, studying civil engineering. We lived fifteen minutes from the university, and he always took the bus early mornings. After he left for school, I couldn't go back to sleep since it was Camii's turn to awaken, and thus, my day began. My husband came home for lunch every day. So, I had to cook in the mornings and make sure lunch was ready at exactly twelve o'clock because after lunch, he went back for his afternoon classes. In the evenings, depending on his academic schedule, sometimes he came home early to share dinner with us, but more often, he came home late after Carmelle was asleep. Loneliness was starting to attack me, but this was a student's wife's life. I knew that. So, I had to do something, and with my husband's encouragement, I went back to school.

Almost a year after I had arrived in Canada, I registered at the University of Sherbrooke in my first math class, a prerequisite to enter into the business administration program. Although school didn't alleviate my domestic responsibilities, I was making sure I was doing something for me as well. That's how I started my second degree. I had tested out the job market and realized that my degree in history from Burundi wasn't in hot demand. I had gone to the University of Sherbrooke's history department to ask whether I could teach African contemporary history (since it was my major), but I was told by the department's director that it would depend on the students' request for such a class. He encouraged me to prepare the curriculum and wait until students would request the class. But I didn't want to waste time preparing a curriculum for a class that wasn't being offered on a regular basis. I decided I would study what my brother Cyriaque had always wanted me to study —economics. But economics in Burundi didn't seem to hold the same meaning as the economics I was about to take in Canada. In Burundi, the economics faculty combined business and economics classes, but put emphasis on micro- and macro-economics. I decided I really wanted to study something that would open up doors for me: business administration. So I applied at the University of Sherbrooke, did all the prerequisites, and got admitted into business administration. It was difficult, to say the least, but I made a commitment to myself that I would continue even if it meant failing some classes and retaking them.

I failed big time a class called "Information Systems" in which I was introduced to computers for the first time. Some of the kids with whom I took the class were experts even in computer programming. They were fresh out of Cégep, the equivalent of a two-year college system after high school. I also struggled with team assignments. In most classes, we had to form teams for group assignments. When the professor said, "Now it's time to form groups of four," all my classmates practically knew each other from their Cégep and would gather with their friends and form instant teams. Shyly, I would ask a team whether they would let me join, but there was no spot left. I would look left, then right, waiting to see whether anyone was left out like me, so we could join forces, but everyone seemed to be part of a team. No one came to me to say, "Do you want to be in our team?" After, the professor would ask, "Is everyone in teams?" Embarrassed, I would raise my hand and tell the teacher that I didn't belong to a team.

Usually, the teacher would ask, "What team doesn't have four members?" and the students would grow silent until the teacher picked up a team for me to join, as their fifth member—an over-age the team didn't really need. Most of these students had lived in Québec all their lives and not even been to Ontario. They weren't used to foreigners that much. So, choosing me, the alien African woman with two kids, just seemed weird to them. Elva, our second daughter had come into the world in September 1994, one year after I had started at the University of Sherbrooke.

Although I was still relatively young at twenty-seven years old when I started at that university, I felt like I was one hundred compared to those teenagers whose average age was nineteen. Being a mother and wife who had to juggle full-time school and family responsibilities, I was simply not an asset for their team. Sometimes, I couldn't understand their French, and they probably didn't understand mine either.

As I advanced to upper grades, I started getting used to the university work, and my grades improved from my usual Cs to B+s, and even occasional As. One of my favorite classes was macroeconomics. I related to this class because it taught global economy, monetary systems, and other fine theories I strived to know. I enjoyed learning the banking system and thought the Canadian banking system was ingenious. Reduced to only six big banks ("the big six") and a few credit unions, it is easy for the Bank of Canada, Canada's central bank, to control the financial institutions and the banking system.

Sometimes, I envied students who only had to put their efforts into studying and didn't have to split their time and energy with the home front. With hard work and determination, I graduated with a bachelor's degree in business administration and a major in finance—just what I wanted. It was quite an accomplishment. And I thought doors would open automatically at my approach.

There were no jobs open for me or for my husband after we both graduated in 1997, so, we decided to move to the big city of Toronto, in the province of Ontario. Toronto is a very big and really a nice clean city. I was first amazed by how diverse the city was. Walking downtown, you could hear five different languages at the same time, any time of the day. The first time I went to the CN

Tower was a true discovery. First, I felt dizzy because of the height and speed, but once I stepped out of the elevator, what a view! I could see Toronto's entire skyline, the Ontario place, Toronto Maple Leaf, Toronto's financial district with its majestic buildings, and much more, all from the tower deck. I instantly fell in love with this city. It felt free and outdoorsy. Later on, I experienced the subway system—quite a learning experience for a girl who had never ridden trains before. I was lost once in the underground while trying to go shopping at a furniture store. I was sure I knew how to get there; I had written down the stops and street names. One morning after my kids left for school (Carmelle was in first grade and Elva in pre-school).

I took the bus to the subway, got on, and was feeling pretty confident. When it was time to get off, I couldn't find my exit. I read the map again and again. The train had completed its trip when I realized I had taken the eastbound train instead of the westbound one. I panicked. How was I going to come back and go home? My kids didn't know I was gone, and there was no one to get them after school. Then I asked another passenger why I didn't see my stop. He showed me how to get back on track and get the westbound train. Needless to say, I didn't make it shopping that day. I was afraid I might get lost again and not make it in time to pick up my kids from school. But, there was a certain thrill in getting lost in the subway, and you were never alone. I later tried again to navigate Toronto by subway and was able to get around pretty easily after my first attempt. I quite enjoyed browsing and shopping at the Toronto Eaton Centre more often. Despite its hugeness, Toronto was a livable city.

Immigrants had more job openings in the customer service field, which was my first job. Those jobs gave us the opportunity to practice English. However, they were not high enough paying jobs to feed a family. In every job I held, I seemed to be overqualified or underemployed. Once I got into a job's routine, I always wanted something more challenging and intellectually stimulating. But, I wasn't alone. The job market was full of smart people, especially those holding business degrees, so no wonder it was hard for me to get into a niche. After a year in Toronto, my husband got a better job in his field and we had to move to Windsor, a city in southern Ontario. I was then pregnant with our third child, which meant I would have to stay home and take care of the baby and our other two kids, while my husband worked to bring home the bacon. This seemed like a perfect family arrangement. We got accustomed to our new area and even bought our first house. Our kids blossomed in Francophone schools, and after the baby was seven months old, I decided to return to work. Again, no big gig for me—just a small job that allowed me to get out of the house, stay on the job market, and be on someone's payroll. I wasn't really looking for a challenging position. With three kids under eight years old (our son Darrel was born when Carmelle was eight in 1999) and a husband who worked so much, there was no room for me to indulge in a career.

Like many North American mothers, I didn't have the luxury of putting my career first so I would be ready to climb the corporate ladder when the time was right. More often than not, I was the one who took time off whenever our kids got sick or could not go to school. This arrangement meant that I only accepted part-time jobs or temporary work, which didn't entitle me to benefits or even boost my resume that much. When I returned to work after maternity leave, I had already been forgotten. I had to start over, which meant entry level jobs again, for which I was overqualified. Sometimes, the work paid me so little that it didn't cover the cost of my working (child care, gas, mileage, even lunch). But it was necessary for me to keep a foot in the door if I wanted to have some meaningful work in the future.

What was more frustrating was that I didn't feel I was accomplishing either role (wife/mother or employee) effectively. I felt trapped in the middle. I knew some mothers were achieving successful careers and motherhood. Oh, God, how did they do it? Trying to fill all the roles drained me, but I was too proud to admit it. On typical days, I would come home from work and start another shift. I would be making dinner while supervising homework and holding my son, who was a very active baby. By the time the kids finally went to bed, I would be dead on my feet. And it was only then that I would hear my husband's key in the door and feel the anger almost choking me. But I was too tired even to argue about his coming home late every night, and I thought it was normal for any good mother or wife to go through this period in her life. Although I felt resentment toward my husband for not helping me with the kids or the house work, I knew a time would come when the kids would be more independent, and maybe one day my husband would realize how much I needed him. I didn't know how to communicate my needs to my husband without breaking down emotionally, which only infused more fights, and no solution to our problems.

I was walking on a mountain of frustration while he worked on a multitude of projects and was busy pleasing other people. At one point, he wasn't even home to share dinners with me anymore, so I became very lonely. But I knew I had to be strong for everyone involved. Fearing I would sink into depression, I started looking for solutions. I visited my first therapist, who counseled me to start taking better care of myself. She told me, "If you're not taking care of yourself, you don't have much to give to anyone else, even your children." That was so true and that's where the challenge was for me. I didn't know how to take care of me without feeling that I was neglecting someone else. Nevertheless, I started with baby steps. My first major improvement was taking "me" time and going to the local library or the book store. That's how I came into contact with self-help books. I started reading them to find inspiration about what to do with all the life confusion I felt. As I regularly browsed through the self-help section of my favorite bookstore in Windsor, called Chapters, I couldn't help but think to myself, "When are you going to stop reading these books, girlfriend?" I became kind of addicted to them.

The self-help books became my best friends and best counselors. After all, they were a lot cheaper than the counseling sessions, and like a good therapist, they offered advice without judgment. For a time, I used to be ashamed of reading self-help books. In my mind, reading them proved that I wasn't strong enough to face life in North America. I was so ashamed of admitting that I needed this kind of emotional boost because I didn't want to acknowledge that I had some issues I needed to work on.

I enjoy reading, but my daughter Elva says that I take my reading a little too far. She is right. I have to confess that sometimes when I am in a bookstore, I would like to read everything I find on the shelves. I inhale the smell of books at Barnes & Noble, and I can sit cross-legged on the floor and read for hours. When I go to the mall, instead of checking out the new season's fashions, I go to the bookstore to check out the newly published books. I have to watch my budget on books; it is my addiction. But Elva says it is a good addiction and that she hopes to have my love of books when she is a grown woman, so I feel better about it.

The encouragement I received from reading self-help books made me decide to join community organizations in Ontario. Because corporate Canada wasn't as open as I had hoped, I thought maybe if I worked with people who shared my dilemma—other immigrant women—I could find a job I would love. I could help myself by helping others and doing meaningful work.

I joined some organizations that worked on resolving issues that held women back: lack of jobs tailored to our needs, lack of support at home, the absentee husbands and fathers, and the different faces of conjugal abuse behind closed doors. I joined organizations such as MOFIF (Ontario Movement for Francophone Immigrant Women) or (*Mouvement Ontarien de Femmes Immigrantes Francophones* in French), a nonprofit organization for French-speaking immigrant women, and CIFODE (*Centre de Formation de Développement Économique*), a nonprofit organization that was working with immigrants to provide professional training for economic development. Both organizations were based in Ottawa at the time. I was a member liaison between the two organizations with another organization I had joined hoping to start an immigrant women's wing of the African-Canadian Community Centre based in Windsor. I worked for ACFO (Canadian-French Association of Ontario) and tried to be involved in our association of Burundians in Windsor as a treasurer.

I was getting immersed in these organizations and loved it. I got invited to roundtables and conferences in Toronto and Ottawa on issues regarding immigrant minorities. I was even defeating my shyness and speaking in public. We worked to find solutions to issues such as the lack of jobs for immigrant men and women who, in most cases, were highly educated and capable. We suggested solutions, mostly asking the Canadian federal government to back us up with professional training programs and policy changes to accommodate these highly educated people.

But policies take time to be implemented, and even more time to bear results. Immigrants also had a load of expectations from back home, where our families need our financial assistance. Besides these general immigrant issues, women had another multitude of problems that added stress to their already stressful lives because they had to adjust to another culture. I felt I needed to do something for the women, and for me. I had the idea to create a mentorship center for immigrant women. But to bring this idea to life, I would need other women to believe in it and to help me build it.

CHAPTER 11 EVOLVING QUESTIONS FOR REFLECTION

1. As an immigrant to a different country and culture, I had to go through some adjustments, and even some deception while trying to fit into my new community. Have you had any similar experiences when adjusting to something new, or do you know someone who has?

_____

_____

_____

_____

_____

2. If so, where did it happen, and how did you or the person(s) you know adjust?

_____

_____

_____

_____

_____

3. Take a moment and reflect on how you can make a difference in a new-comer's life. What advice would you give to someone who immigrates to a different country where everything is different from what he/she is used to?

_____

_____

_____

_____

_____

Chapter 12

COMMEMORATING INTERNATIONAL WOMEN'S DAY

Leadership is action, not position.
—Donald H. McGannon

As a new comer, I felt that part of my isolation was because we immigrants were disconnected from the communities we lived in. So in March of 2003, I had an idea for how to celebrate International Women's Day. I thought if I could organize something that could bring people together: immigrants and local, provincial, and federal government representatives, we could talk, have fun, and get to know each other. I organized the event with the help of a group of immigrant women from Burundi, Rwanda, and the Congo. We put together poetry, music, and dance. Food was catered by the community center, which agreed to rent us its space. I got Rwandan kids to perform their traditional dances, which are always a delight to watch. With space, food, music, dancing and participants, I was all set to prepare the speeches in English and French. I wanted our non-French speakers to be included. I crafted invitations on a word processor and wrote the speeches on my computer at home. I invited Honorable Member of Federal Parliament (MP) Susan Whelan (my town belonged to her constituency). I also sent an invitation to the Ontario Minister of Social Services and Member of Provincial Parliament (MPP) Sandra Pupatello, and many other community leaders. I contacted the media, and the local Canadian Broadcasting Corporation (CBC) television station agreed to come and see whether there was any interesting news to cover. Because of the dignitaries I had invited, CBC came.

On March 8, 2003, I woke up at 7 a.m, got ready, and put on my Burundi ceremonial attire. I had everything set up; I had rehearsed my speeches in both English and French, and I had called everyone who needed to be called. We were ready to kick off some fun on International Women's Day. I was a little anxious about the turnout, but I had never seen such an attendance. Men, women, children, and everyone in between came dressed in their favorite colorful outfits, as if going to a great ceremony, and they were on time! Not African time, but North American time. I was almost floating with pride that my people didn't let me down. A family friend had agreed to film the event for free, so that was another service I didn't have to pay for. Everyone was so beautiful; my heart was pounding with gratitude for the people who showed up.

After everybody was settled, the master of ceremonies introduced the event and the respective speakers. I was to be the first major speaker with my bilingual speech carefully placed in my folder. Trying to appear calm and collected, I went to the podium. As I spoke my opening lines, my voice began to betray me. I could hear myself starting to shake as if my throat were squeezed and no air…no air. I tried to clear it, but the shaking in my voice became consistent as if I might cry. "Oh, please, God, help me. I don't want to cry in front of these people; I am the one who started this whole thing and invited them. They could be somewhere else, you know. But they chose to come and give me a chance, and hear what the fuss is all about. Please, help my voice be strong and keep my emotions in check, okay?"

As I pleaded with God, I felt a certain calmness—I felt held together. I started to recognize the invitees: "Honorable Susan Whelan, honorable community leaders representing your respective organizations, brothers and sisters …we are here today to celebrate International Women's Day." Then I tried to lighten up the atmosphere, braced myself, and said, "I am sorry you missed your morning nap this Saturday; you can blame it on me." People laughed and some even applauded. And that really did it! I felt the energy lift. So, I talked about the meaning of such a day for myself and many other women across the globe. I cited all the important men and women who had suffered hardships before us to make sure women could vote, go to school, and occupy important positions in government or private sectors. I talked about Harriet Tubman, who had made thirteen missions to rescue slaves, using the network of antislavery activists and safe houses, all better known as the underground railroad. I cited all the important women and men who had helped shape the history of women's rights. They were the reason we celebrated International Women's Day.

Then, I turned to issues that needed more work to ensure that women could claim an even better future for themselves, be less financially dependent, and be treated less like second class citizens in their own homes and communities. These were the most important reasons why I had been compelled to organize this day. As I talked about how immigrant women were being badly treated by those who should be their protectors, namely their husbands, my voice trailed off again, and I choked up a little. "Oh, God, please; I can't afford to cry here; I am at the podium for goodness' sake!" I took one deep breath, as if oxygen might be unavailable for the next twenty-four hours, and smoothly, I exhaled. I felt a peaceful breeze as I continued my speech with even more vigor in my voice. I could see the audience was moved. The high-ranking officials tried not to show emotions, but I could feel them closer to me; I could tell everyone was touched by my speech.

As I concluded, thanking all of them for coming, I had never felt so proud of myself. The message to take home was, "Let's work together for immigrant women's advancement, and let's make it a societal issue and not an individual issue." The day in itself was to evaluate how far we had come and how far we could go. The ceremonies served as a bonding opportunity with all members of the communities we lived in. It helped to raise awareness that most immigrant women were isolated and lonely; some of them didn't even speak English, and they needed to feel they belonged. I thanked the audience again and returned to my seat.

I had prepared an evaluation questionnaire, so at the end of the ceremonies, people wrote their feedback about the day. I wanted to learn what we did right and what we could improve. The general feedback was amazing. People were very happy about the turn-out and demanded that next year it be longer. I had been afraid that people might be impatient or bored, but they stayed till the end of the event. Susan Whelan had other commitments and left after her speech. As I accompanied her outside when she left, she thanked me and all the women who had made this day possible and even praised my efforts as an organizer. I thanked her in return for taking time from her busy schedule as an MP to attend our event. MPP Pupatello could not come, but she sent us her best wishes and a congratulatory letter to let us know she was with us even if she couldn't be there. This was my first time being in close contact with people in politics such as MPs and MPPs. That evening, CBC aired our event with a five-minute segment in its news broadcast. I was ecstatic!

After my stint in that event, I understood well the job description of an organizer. Although it seemed like it was what I would like to do when I grew up, it couldn't pay my bills. I understood the frustration of those who did it for a living, and how one got tired too quickly and even aged faster compared to their non- organizer counterparts. I was working part- time at a bank for an intern's salary, despite my business degree. There was no way being an organizer could have helped me achieve a better income, but it was the work I enjoyed the most.

I continued my involvement in the community, mostly volunteering with other established organizations. These organizations suffered from a lack of necessary funding to accommodate their budgets. Immigrants seemed to fight for the few available jobs within these non-profit immigrant organizations. If you didn't show them the money, you shouldn't expect them to support your fancy ideas; people had families to feed and were fed up with how they felt unworthy of anything. They had left their war-torn countries for a better life. In some cases, men didn't appreciate that their women expected them to help with dishes, or God forbid, change baby diapers; and consequently, anger and resentment led to women battering and other abusive behaviors.

CHAPTER 12 EVOLVING QUESTIONS FOR REFLECTION

1. Take a moment and list the many ways you can make the world a better place.

_____

_____

_____

_____

_____

2. What gifts and talents do you have that you can share with others?

_____

_____

_____

_____

_____

3. What's your passion in life? Spend some time exploring where your passion meets the needs of this world.

_____

_____

_____

_____

_____

Chapter 13

CHASING THE
AMERICAN DREAM

All human beings are also dream beings.
Dreaming ties all mankind together.
—Jack Kerouac

In 2004, my family relocated to Michigan, a state at the border of the Canadian province of Ontario. We moved from the city of Windsor where we had been living for six years. Windsor is so geographically close to the American city of Detroit that you could just merge the two into one. Only separated by the Detroit River, it takes about ten minutes to go from one city to the other, either through the tunnel or over the Ambassador Bridge. Economically, Windsor is an automotive extension of Michigan; most people in Windsor work in the automotive industry and depend on it. When this industry was hit by an economic crisis, Windsor automotive manufacturers were the first to lay-off auto workers, which placed tremendous hardship on many families.

After my trials and errors in Canada, I saw the chance to come to America as a self-rescue mission. After all, I had learned of "The American Dream" back in high school, when our geography teacher, Mr. Alphonse, would tell us about America being a melting pot.

The words had been ingrained in my brain ever since, and when I came to America, I realized what "melting pot" meant. While I have no statistics in front of me, I believe every country in the world is represented by someone living in the United States of America. But here, too, my fantasies did not instantly materialize. I got my share of lengthy unemployment time following the financial crisis and the bailout era. I, too, was affected by the automotive industry crash, followed by the real estate crisis. For more than three years, I had only contract positions and my American Dream included a huge mortgage for a house we could barely afford.

After we settled into our suburban life, I sought out how I could continue my community organization endeavors in the Detroit area. I wanted to join something that would help me and my family adjust, fit in, and belong. I researched organizations in the area where we lived, thirty miles north west of Detroit. It was a nice suburb that was mainly white, but had attracted some African-American families in their quest for better-funded schools for their kids. In my search, I found a nonprofit organization that seemed to be what I was looking for. I emailed the secretary to tell her I was interested in participating in their events, and she advised me to attend their next meeting, which was being held at a local school.

The meeting was attended by African-Americans, both men and women, who were part of the working class, mostly middle-aged, and college-educated. The meeting was about how African-American kids were progressing in math and the sciences. As each parent spoke of his or her concerns about African-American kids, how they weren't doing well in math for instance; someone mentioned that it was due to a syndrome he called the "I have arrived syndrome." African-Americans who had moved to the suburbs from Detroit, suffered from this syndrome, the participant said. "Once they move away from the hoods to where schools are well-funded, parents of African-American kids stop worrying about their sons' education because they think it's taken care of by teachers and school administrators. They think they have arrived." I thought to myself," Wow! I've Arrived Syndrome? How brilliant!" He said parents stopped going to parent-teacher conferences, so they didn't know what their children were learning anymore.

Someone started projecting fancy statistics that showed the standard deviations within school demographics in the U.S. "God, don't you know how I hate statistics?" I muttered to myself. After I assessed the meeting in my head, although the issues were all too familiar, I wasn't ready for this kind of serous involvement. I decided to take time first to get acquainted with my immediate living space. I needed to know how to get to the grocery stores, the malls, and all the places that help you spend money. Most importantly, I craved books. I had to find bookstores and self-indulge.

The books I read, especially those in my favorite self-help category, each taught me something special about myself, my values, and what I stand for. They inspired me to stand up for myself and what I value when no one else would. I value integrity, honesty, and equality. Each book I read promised me something—that I, too, was entitled to happiness and that I was the one to look out for myself, especially by being clear about what I wanted. I knew I had to change something in my life, but I didn't know what it was, or how to go about changing it. Isn't it ironic that we tend to know what we don't want rather than what we do want? A friend told me one day that she knew what kind of man she didn't want. I said, "Uhum…aren't you supposed to know the opposite? I mean, what kind of man you want instead? "

When he was eight years old, my son Darrel once asked me, "Mom, what do you wanna be?"

"Maybe a finance person sweetie," I mumbled, unconvinced myself.

"Oh, okay!" my son said. I can't believe he bought that because I didn't feel very confident when I said it. I tried to persuade him that I was trying to be a somebody out there, and my son had no problem believing me, but I was the one who didn't believe in myself. I had that nasty little voice ringing in my head telling me that I would never amount to anything; that I wasn't ambitious enough to deserve a better career. "Look at you," the voice would say. "You have three degrees, but what have you done with them, huh, huh?" All my inner bullies just made me feel unworthy and stuck.

One reason for that feeling was that I craved love, affection, and appreciation and always tried to "buy" that love by doing what others wanted me to do. Another was that I analyzed my life through other people's successes and not through my own. Why wasn't I on a fast-track career path like others who held master's degrees? However, all that arguing with myself didn't help me get clarity on what I was supposed to do to get ahead in my career.

As I continued to stalk Monster and CareerBuilder websites, I was discouraged. The more I searched for jobs, the less clear I was about what I truly wanted to do. With all my degrees, my skills, and my talents, I didn't just want a job—I wanted *the* job. I know this sounds weird, but I didn't know what *the* job looked like. What scared me more was that *the* job and I could have met, and I didn't recognize it.

I was going through this struggle five months before I was to turn forty. Yeah, that tricky age—forty. The midlife crisis was my own assessment. But I knew there was no turning back the clock. What's wrong with turning forty anyway? For one thing, turning forty makes you think about your own purpose in life on this Earth.

A certain self-awareness becomes undeniable. I am sure there is a better name for this stage in life besides midlife crisis.

When I got past this crisis, I entered stage two of my self-analysis about my life from birth to age forty. Who was I in my family? In my relationships, why was I compromising so much? But there is nothing wrong with compromising if you know who you are, and you are not compromising your values. I realized I didn't understand myself that much; nor did I love myself as I should from my inner-self.

As I analyzed my career path, I found that I was rather inclined to apply and get jobs for which I was overqualified. After three months on the job, I would be frustrated because I wasn't using my educational skills. Next, I would leave those jobs to enter yet another of the same caliber, just in a different company that promised me growth, only to see how difficult it was to climb the ladder. I remember a certain gentleman from a recruitment agency that was helping me to look for a job, asking me a rather painful question. "Seconde, with all your credentials," he said, "why have you worked only in entry level positions?"

"The jobs I've held in the past have all taught me something new, and had I stayed longer in those jobs, maybe something better would have come out of it," I told him. It was my rehearsed answer that I had given many times. But inside, my nagging voice was berating me. "Say the truth, girl; you are an underachiever. Just admit it!"

In my own right, I have come to understand why I applied for and accepted less satisfying jobs. First, they were the easiest to get, and secondly, it was due to my family situation. I cared about money and position of course, but I was always afraid that a good position would require greater time commitment, and I would end up neglecting my family. So, like a runaway bride, I was always running away from getting good jobs or not staying long enough in the jobs I held to wait for the opportunity to arrive. As I reached my forties, I looked back at my accomplishments—yes, I was proud of my children and what I had given to my family, and I was proud of my higher education, but my career path was a mess! I had no retirement fund of my own; I was always dependent on my husband's salary. I had given up pursuing a career because I wanted our family to have a high quality of life but then I hadn't carved out any financial security for myself.

As I had done before whenever I felt confusion, I turned to my only nonjudgmental friends: the books. Any free time I had was spent at Borders, before it went out of business. I came across *Your Best Life Now* by Joel Osteen, a book I read in my quest for solutions to my dilemma. I also read the journal that goes with it, in which you can do some practical exercises. Joel Osteen is a minister from Houston who writes about believing in God to improve our lives. The day I discovered that book, it gave me some energy I was lacking, and it taught me to be grateful for what I had, instead of what I should have. I stopped profiling myself as an underachiever or less than ambitious because my ego was telling me that. I started to realize where I had come from. Many people were living in extreme poverty, here or elsewhere in the world, so my situation wasn't that bad after all. I started to learn how to appreciate myself and be grateful for who I was as a person.

It was then that the job I held started to provide me with satisfaction. I had started that job with a high school intern's salary. But once I started appreciating it, my salary was increased, in small increments, but steadily, three times in two years. I didn't realize I was getting salary increases at that speed until I started to enjoy myself and love myself for who I was. I started indulging the little girl in me, who was craving love and attention without knowing that the best love was to come from within.

Although self-love didn't fix all my problems, it helped me to acknowledge them and eventually face them. I started taking a close look at my marriage to understand why it wasn't satisfying. In meetings and roundtables with women organizations, and even with friends, I encouraged others to stand up for themselves, but I wasn't doing that in my personal life. Because I didn't like conflicts, I had become a doormat and anybody could have walked all over me. Having this realization was the most difficult but most enlightening time in my life. Basically, I realized that I was the one who would have to make changes if I wanted things to be different. But how do you make changes? It wasn't easy, but I knew that sooner or later, it would be up to me to face the situation and honor my true self.

CHAPTER 13 EVOLVING QUESTIONS FOR REFLECTION

1. Take a moment and reflect on your dreams.

_____

_____

_____

_____

_____

2. Which dreams do you hold dear and what are you doing to make them come true?

_____

_____

_____

_____

_____

3. If you have had a dream come true, what lesson(s) have you learned from achieving it?

_____

_____

_____

_____

_____

Chapter 14

BREAKING THE CYCLE

Remember always that you not only have the right to be an individual; you have an obligation to be one.
—Eleanor Roosevelt

"Oh, God, I am one of them now. I made the statistics. Another divorce has been filed and increased the divorce rate in America because of me." Those were the thoughts racing through my mind as I was going through my divorce. In many cultures and religions, divorce is a sin. And in the culture I come from, this sin is even more punishable for women. When a man is the one who leaves his marriage, people don't go around judging him as much as they do women no matter the circumstances. Therefore, conventional traditions do not provide any suggestions for what to do if a woman is suffocated in a marriage, other than to accept her situation. The term "niko zubakwa" literally meaning "suck it up" in Kirundi, illustrates that other married women go through bad treatments, so you're not the only one, and therefore, why should you complain?

In Burundi, traditional marriages were blessed as two families came together—cows were gifted to the future bride's family, and later, marriage was consummated. The girl would leave her family and neighbors and go to live with her husband's family where she would be the wife and be expected to bear children as soon as the bells rang for the end of the wedding ceremony.

When I was a little girl, but not so little not to understand adult conversations, I used to listen to Barenga, my adopted aunt, and her friends talk about someone they knew who got married. I would hear them talk about the battle of the nuptials. How the bride had been scared, how she lost her virginity, and all the details I didn't want to know because I would get so disgusted that I vowed never to get married. It sounded painful as they went on and on talking. However, they seemed to be at ease and quite envious of the married girl they talked about. The most unforgettable story I would hear was about a man who was "unable" to perform the task of making his bride lose her virginity. In cases like these, there was so much to talk about. It seemed as if everybody in the village knew what had happened to the poor fellow and his new wife. When I was in high school, our Kirundi class teacher used to tell us that in traditional marriages, there were people who snuck behind the newlyweds' house to listen to their first sexual act. That's how those who weren't able to "perform" were reported. It made the talk of the village for months; tabloids are everywhere!

As far as I was concerned, sex education was mostly done by Barenga. She taught me much of what I knew until further details were acquired in high school from friends and biology classes (particularly the chapter on human reproduction). Barenga was the one who informed me about girls menstruating, and why it happened. She called it "*kuja mu kwezi*" ("going into the moon") because menstruations happen once a month, and the months were counted by full moons, the equivalent of a lunar calendar. Barenga used to tell me, "At around twelve years old, you may see blood come out of your girly parts."

"Why?" I would inquire with worried eyes at the mention of blood.

"Because God created a girl to become a woman, and to bear children," she would say. But I couldn't make the connection between having children and the bleeding part. Then she would go on telling me that bleeding each month was a way of preparing a girl for womanhood. She taught me more than my own mother did on the subject. As a matter of fact, my mother never taught me anything about sex. Sex education wasn't part of how parents raised their children. It was a taboo subject and we kids kept to ourselves whatever information we had about sex. However, by the time I went to live with my parents, I knew a lot, thanks to Barenga. For a woman who never went to school, she was awfully smart.

After a girl became a woman and somebody's wife, tradition made it seem natural that whatever happened in the marriage should stay in the marriage. If a woman were unfortunate and had a bad marriage, she was never to complain about it or tell anybody she was unhappy. Her parents expected her to be on her best behavior because she was considered the ambassador of her own family to the family of her husband. And when I say family, it's beyond Mom and Dad or even Grandma and Grandpa. Family in Burundi is way larger than the mere limits of the relatives of your own generation. This structure is very constructive in many ways. Families help each other because if you look back into your family tree, the person you help might be related to you in the nth generation and is still called family. There is no such thing as "removed" relatives. Therefore, when you get married, you bring two large families together from previous generations to future generations. It is a big responsibility to bear, and no one in either family needs to know you are not happy in your marriage, or what's happening unless it's all good.

When it was my time to be wed, I didn't have any special knowledge about marriage, nor did I have a good role model to emulate. I didn't get any "marriage training." And this was a modern wedding, if I may brag. I had a white dress and everything. No one made me marry my husband; I consented with all my heart. I had my family's blessings and his family accepted me as one of theirs. Therefore, when we started having difficulties in our marriage, I kept it to myself. Neither my husband nor I had any idea how to manage our adversities, except to fight, or just retreat into other projects and avoid each other. We didn't have any communication skills when it came to our relationship conflicts, and we didn't know how to ask for help. I couldn't tell anyone in our respective families that we were having problems in our marriage because they viewed us as the perfect couple. And even those I finally told when I couldn't take it anymore, checked the information with my husband because they didn't believe me. He assured them that everything was fine, and our problems were only the normal interactions between husband and wife. So, for a long time, I didn't want to challenge that status quo.

In 2007, my brother Cyriaque became the first person in my family to know my husband and I had marital troubles and were on the verge of divorce. As soon as he learned about it, he wrote me an email in which he said things I never dreamt he would say to me. After that, we did not speak for almost six months. My brother never asked me what had happened. He only knew one-sided version of the story. This was very devastating to me, as my brother and I had always been close. I felt betrayed beyond words because Cyriaque wasn't just my brother, he was my best friend. When I had started living with my parents permanently, Cyriaque had instantly become my closest sibling (He is two years older than me). When we were both in high school, we used to have intellectual conversations; he liked to quiz me with math games since he was a nerd in math, and I would test his French knowledge and pronunciation. Therefore, all the years I hadn't spoken to my brother about my marriage being in trouble, had been mostly so I wouldn't disappoint him. Despite how close Cyriaque and I were, I knew I would be the one to be blamed; the woman is always at fault.

In addition, my immediate family had high hopes for me as the only girl who had achieved higher education and been to Canada and America. That created an additional burden for me to provide for my extended family. I was Cyriaque's financial backup to help our aging parents, our siblings and our other relatives. It was understandable that my brother was concerned by my divorce. It didn't take long before others who heard about it joined together in judging me. To many who knew my husband and I as a couple, we didn't fit the profile of the "divorcing type," so they were surprised.

I realized that neither I, nor my husband, knew how to save our marriage after it had been tested time and again. Having been both students at one point, we had moved on to being parents to three children without any adequate finances to take care of them. So we blamed each other instead of finding a common ground and solutions. And when we started working, our jobs and our family responsibilities took precedence over our relationship. It was too difficult for me to wear a mask any longer and pretend we were a happy couple, as we had done in the name of pleasing others. I had overlooked many things in our marriage for a long time, mainly to not disappoint other people. But I had to rise above all judgments and break the cycle. As I went through the difficult times, I also rediscovered my strengths.

CHAPTER 14 EVOLVING QUESTIONS FOR REFLECTION

1. Have you ever gone through a divorce? If so, how was your experience and what did it teach you about yourself?

_____

_____

_____

_____

_____

2. If you have had or still have a healthy marriage, or you experienced what a good marriage is through your parents or other people, what do you think is the secret to a good marriage?

_____

_____

_____

_____

_____

3. What is your advice to young people in regards to healthy marriages and strong families?

_____

_____

_____

_____

_____

Chapter 15

SURVIVING TOUGH TIMES

Courage is grace under pressure.
—Ernest Hemingway

After I went through all the inevitable loneliness that crept in following my divorce, I started to realize I had kept my misery to myself most of the time, and that the whining had subsided. I vowed to myself that I would never jump into a relationship just to fill the void. Of that much, I was certain. Besides, I didn't have too much time to indulge myself since I had the overwhelming responsibilities of single parenting. I was living in Michigan alone with the kids (their father had already relocated to Washington State for a new job). I had to split myself to assume many roles. I had to motivate the girls to work hard at school, help my son with homework, attend parent-teacher meetings, drop the kids off at school when they had missed the school bus, take them to doctors' appointments, and all the while, work at a full-time job as a contract employee.

That winter of 2008, I had never seen so much snow in Michigan. My driveway was a constant stressor. Fortunately, I had kind neighbors who took on removing the snow from my driveway with a snow blower every morning before I was even awake. I am very grateful to Renee and Steve Samp for their kindness; they helped me when I most needed it. It seemed that every snowstorm was followed by ice storms, and some days, my car couldn't move on the icy driveway. Then my other neighbors, Paul and Debbie Kin, became my good Samaritans. Because of the bad weather, the kids were constantly sick, and I was constantly called from work to come and pick them up from school. When Darrel got sick right after Elva got better, I had to call my manager and tell her I couldn't go to work. She suggested I hire a sitter to look after my sick child. How could I leave a sick child in the care of a sitter? I stayed home. I had started that job after a seven-month unemployment period, and I was determined to excel at it, and hopefully, land a permanent placement in the company. But being absent right after I had started working was not proving my intentions to work hard. The manager was very patient with me. I went through rigorous training with tight deadlines. It was a multitasking, detail-oriented, number-crunching, spreadsheet job, which added to my chaotic personal life.

Now from the outside, you wouldn't have been able to tell my life was so chaotic. Even my kids never noticed that their mom was extended beyond her 5' 3". One day in March of 2008, as my son Darrel was recuperating, Carmelle injured her neck on the icy roads running to catch her school bus in the dark morning. I was called yet again to come and pick her up from school, and take her to the doctor. At that point, my super-woman powers had worn off. I was worn out. Some mornings, I would drive to work, wondering whether I had just gone through red lights or whether they had turned green. I couldn't remember. I would look in the rear view mirror to see whether other cars had followed me. Thank God, they had! Other times, I felt as if I were floating on autopilot while driving on the highway to work, and I would wonder whether I had just taken the wrong exit. My health was deteriorating, my immune system was wearing down, and that meant I caught every cold circulating at work or at home. My manager continued to be very understanding and patient. She appreciated my dedication and hard work, but she was worried about my not meeting tight deadlines because of time taken off to care for the kids. Catching up with reporting deadlines after a day's absence became my constant battle.

One night, after I went to bed, I sat down and assessed my situation. Here I was with a new and demanding job, and I wasn't feeling well or available enough to commit to making it a career. My work ethic has always been to do the best I could and master the job quickly until I could do it with eyes closed. That had always been the case with my previous jobs because I had always gone for the less challenging. But in this job, there was a real challenge. I was used to mastering a job in only three months, but for this one, I needed at least twelve months. Each time I got one task mastered, there were three others I needed to learn. I didn't want to admit it, but I felt that either my career was failing me or the reverse. Once again, I had to choose between career achievement and family, and this time, as a divorced African woman. I knew I would have to relocate to Washington State when my kids started summer vacations so they could be near their father. The next day, I knew what I needed to do. I went to work and asked to meet my manager.

We sat down in a private office where I explained my situation and how I wasn't doing my best in the job because of my absences due to my family circumstances. She completely understood, but she had no idea what was coming next. "I don't feel I am contributing enough to my work due to personal issues," I told her. "I have to step down from this job so it can be available to someone who's able to do it at 100 percent." As I spoke, tears started welling and spilling down my cheeks. She understood and wished me well. She also told me that I had stayed in that job longer than anyone who had held it before me. Because it was during the economic crash and the resulting turmoil, the company had laid-off many employees and their duties had been reassigned to the people who stayed. That meant one person would do three people's jobs, and that was the case with my contract position. Although I was full of regret for another missed career opportunity, I was confident in my decision to put my family first, even if no one would praise me for it. I instantly missed the money I was making, but being available for my kids during this transitioning time in our lives, proved to be important to me.

After the divorce was official, there was no denial anymore. I had to assume responsibility for what I must have done to allow my marriage to fall apart. And yes, I pleaded guilty on several counts. The first count was my inability to express my own needs and stand firm. During our first six years of marriage, I had played the "good wife" who didn't like to complain about things. Growing up in a home where I had witnessed too much strife, I was determined to avoid falling into the same pattern. So, there were things my husband did that made me unhappy, but I had chosen to keep them to myself from fear that we might fight about it. And when I started complaining, he didn't understand why, all of a sudden, I was unhappy about things that had occurred so many times before. And the fights I had so desperately avoided, now started to heat up and it was very tough to give in again, so our fights stayed unsettled. As life went on for another ten years, other issues had been added that stayed unsettled time and time again until my emotional backlog became unbearable.

During my self-analysis, I wondered why, in the beginning, I had always been the one who gave in. What was wrong with me that made me want to avoid conflicts at all costs? I acknowledged that if I had stood my ground from the start, maybe those things my husband and I had fought about would have stopped. But then, I had been afraid that my not agreeing to everything would have resulted in a divorce. Divorce wasn't what I wanted. I wanted peace and harmony and a fulfilling relationship. But I wasn't equipped to ask for what I needed. Our issues followed us everywhere we lived because we never acknowledged them in order to deal with them. Sometimes, I think marriage counseling would have helped our marriage if we both had been willing participants. However, marriage counseling is not everyone's cup of tea. Some people are against counseling, and you can't force them against their will. First of all, many people think of marriage counseling as a guilt confession, where you talk about your marital problems. Marriage counseling is more beneficial when both can attend. Counselors don't necessarily have to be psychologists. It can be your pastor, your priest, or anyone who is qualified in marriage counseling. You might be intimidated by counseling, but believe me, it's better to take action than not.

In my self-analysis, I also understood that I didn't speak up be-cause I wanted my husband to love me more than I loved myself. I attributed this fact to being raised by elderly grandparents, who had been my caretakers first, but when they became older and less mobile, I took on the caretaking role. They had scratched my back so to speak, and later, it became my turn to scratch theirs. Before my grandmother died, she could barely talk because of her asthma, and my grandfather had broken his hips and needed help getting up on his walker. This entire care-taking business left me with an affection deficit. I wasn't connected to my own parents because

I only started living with them after the age of twelve. Instead, I always felt a void had been left after my grandmother died.

Stephen R. Covey, in his book *The 7 Habits of Highly Effective People* uses the term "emotional bank account" in connection with relationships. In my case, when I married, I thought it would be my chance to stock up my "affection bank account" and fill up my emotional void. After all, I thought marriage was meant to do just that. I can see now that I was asking too much, but I would still argue that a marriage, to be fulfilling or at least to survive, has to include a certain amount of attention, affection, and appreciation. But I wasn't equipped to ask for what I needed. I expected my husband to read my mind and say, "Oh, honey, I am so sorry I have neglected you all these years, while I was busy pleasing other people." I have to admit, I really wanted him to come to me and recognize that he was withdrawing from my "emotional bank account" and forgetting to make a deposit. I had to learn the hard way how to value myself instead of expecting someone else to do the work.

I have become a great fan of experts who promote good self-talk. Really, what you tell yourself in your thoughts is what will be projected on the outside. Evolving from a shy personality, I had a hard time promoting a confident me. Loving myself was quite an undertaking because somewhere in the course of my life, I had lost perspective of who I was, and what I stood for. And this lost perspective had cost me a lot in many instances. I had a hard time acknowledging what my worth was or what I deserved. Even in the divorce proceedings, I conceded in many areas because I felt I didn't deserve better. I kept thinking that eventually someone would notice how much I had given to the marriage and to my family, and give me credit.

During my inner search and self-discovery, I learned a few things about myself. As a woman, I had made some mistakes, and one of them was going into a relationship as a dependent person. As I shared earlier, I was eight months pregnant when I got married. I was in my last year of university, so I was still a student and basically a kid, but age had nothing to do with it. I was old enough to get married, but young enough to wait. Neither my husband nor I were ready to settle down, but we were already expecting. I was not only financially dependent; I was also emotionally dependent and full of many fantasies about marriage. As a result, I turned a blind eye on many of the things I didn't like in the relationship, and I also did what many women do—I thought I could change my husband after we were married. When that didn't work, I lowered my standards because I was afraid to stand up for myself. I lacked self-esteem when I entered the relationship, and I hoped it was up to my husband to value me. I learned the hard way to accept myself for who I am, flaws and all, and put aside my false expectations.

CHAPTER 15 EVOLVING QUESTIONS FOR REFLECTION

1. Can you reflect on a time when you faced a life test?

_____

_____

_____

_____

_____

2. What was the situation, and how did you manage it?

_____

_____

_____

_____

_____

3. What lessons did you learn from this situation, and how did those lessons help you in the future?

_____

_____

_____

_____

_____

Chapter 16

HONORING TRUE SELF

*Most of the shadows of this life are caused by our standing in
our own sunshine.*
—Ralph Waldo Emerson

After I agreed that the children and I would move to Seattle
where my ex-husband had been living for a year, I started feeling
distraught about the moving costs, packing, and all that goes along
with moving. One day, I was feeling particularly down because I
didn't have any income. My ex-husband had said that we would
pack our belongings in a U-Haul truck and drive from Detroit to
Seattle. Just thinking about driving such a long distance left me exhausted. One morning, I felt so confused and drained that I didn't
know what to do. So I went in my room and lay down on my bed,
facing the ceiling. I started counting all my miseries: Why did I
have to move again? Why did I have to be the one who always had
to pack? And, of course, I started that terrible sobbing.

Fortunately, my kids were at school, and no one was home but
me. For about five minutes, I cried hot tears, choking on words as I
asked God to help me be clear on what to do. I think He must have
heard me and answered right away. Before I knew it, I started read-

ing Eckhart Tolle's *A New Earth: Awakening to Your Life's Purpose* that I had kicked on the floor in my bedroom a while before. Mr. Tolle hadn't given me the answers I needed quickly enough, so I had thrown the book on the floor beside my bed. I had started reading the book when Oprah had started her online class on the book with Tolle. I had read about the ego, and now I was up to Chapter Five where Tolle talks about "being free." But that morning, I hadn't wanted to read the book; it was only reminding me that I was unhappy (yeah, because I needed a reminder).

But when I asked God to guide me, I blew my nose, wiped my tears, and felt a strong pull toward *A New Earth*. I picked up the book and read pages 165 and 166, where there was the story of a woman who came to see Mr. Tolle. She was so unhappy about her past, especially her childhood. Eckhart Tolle told her to stop and feel the pain. I understood that passage as his asking her to stop resisting the "pain-body" (as he calls it in the book) and actually feel it. At that particular time, I had an Aha! moment. That passage gave me the answers I was looking for. God had just guided me as I had asked Him to. He had guided me toward that passage in Mr. Tolle's book. What I learned was that I didn't have to resist my unhappiness; I just had to accept it, and that meant accepting my confusion, my loneliness, and my sadness about my failed marriage.

These were normal feelings to have, and I didn't need to resist them. I then jotted down a sentence in my journal that said, "I don't mind moving to Seattle and I don't mind not moving to Seattle." I felt so released right away. I opened my bedroom window to let the ugliness of my negative energy go away (I read about this too in the same chapter). I stood up, put my socks on, changed into my gym clothes and walking shoes, and went for a walk in my neighborhood. It was a breezy, sunny April day, so beautiful that I felt reenergized. But I could only feel this breezy, sunny day after all the motions I just described above. When I was feeling tense and miserable, there was no sun. I felt chilly, but it was warm and sunny outside. I just didn't want to feel it.

Once I accepted my "unhappiness," I, too, like the woman in Mr. Tolle's book, "felt room around my unhappiness." Once I accepted that I didn't mind moving if there were resources to achieve the move, and that I also didn't mind not moving if that were the universe's plan, I was released from all expectations. I was in the moment where I was sure that this day was a pretty day, and I shouldn't waste it crying over a moving situation I couldn't control.

Another revelation I got that day was that, as a parent, and now a divorced one, I needed to learn how to be gentle toward myself. I had enough people judging me already, so I needed to be on my side for once. I started learning that I should not only take care of my kids, but also take care of myself. I'd always had difficulties in this arena. I tended to think that taking care of me means abandoning somebody else. I kept waiting for someone to say, "Sweetie, you have been taking care of everybody else. Why don't you start taking care of yourself?" I waited for a permission slip to be signed, but, of course, it never happened. If anything, my caring load only increased because I was always available for others. That is something I have had to work on and be very vigilant about. Some days I can master it, and other days I can't.

I used to be a nutcase. For instance, if I took an hour away from home to go to the library, I used to feel my kids might resent me. I realized that it wasn't anyone in my care who made me feel guilty; it was me. I had suffered what I perceived as abandonment in my early years when I was prematurely severed from my mother and sent to my grandparents, but my psyche had never made the distinction between being abandoned, and being cared for by other people, other than my parents. I transposed this psyche in my adult life, which said, "If you're not here in person, then you must have abandoned me." Therefore, if I wasn't physically there for my kids or my husband, I felt guilty, as if I had abandoned them. That belief, I thought, made me a good companion, but did my husband need this close companionship as much as I did? Probably not. And when it came to the kids, my guilt was even greater. Because I perceived that I had been abandoned, I didn't want my children to feel the same. So, I felt guilty for taking time off for myself, or going back to work, or whatever made me physically absent from their scene. Did the kids mind a few hours alone when they were sufficiently grown and able to be by themselves? Of course not!

While this abandonment issue of mine made things difficult for me, it also strengthened me to be a present person, a physically and emotionally available person. Now, I am not saying I am a better or worse person than anyone else; every personality trait has its advantages and disadvantages. One needs only to appreciate those traits and learn to live with them. I thank God for this awareness and self-acceptance. I vowed to stay true to who I am, so that whoever loves me, loves the person they meet and see. I've never succeeded in hiding my emotions anyway. What you see is what you get.

A couple of months after my divorce, although I kept my resentment in control, there was something that kept bothering me. I didn't like the silent treatment my family in Burundi was giving me. I told a cousin of mine, who lives in America, how angry I was at my brother for never giving me the chance to explain why I had opted out of my marriage. He only knew the version told by my ex-husband, which explained why my brother was hurt. But my cousin kept encouraging me to call my folks in Burundi, saying that they didn't understand what we Burundians went through here in America without any family support. They expect us to live the American Dream. I understood how blessed I was to live in America, and that I should never take it for granted, but still…I needed my family's unconditional support and love, married or divorced, living in America or elsewhere.

My cousin even bought me numerous phone cards that provided hours of talk time, but I was too hurt to initiate a conversation with my family. After a while, however, I realized that my resentment was only hurting me, and not them. In reality, they had moved on and weren't losing any sleep over my divorce. I had wished to have them envelope me with warm hugs, but again, I learned the hard way that my expectations were unrealistic. I learned that I had to be the one to accept myself as I am. I prayed day and night to be able to forgive my family for not taking a stand for me, and slowly, I started feeling released from my anger.

One day, out of the blue, I received an email from Cyriaque saying that our mother was visiting him where he lived in Bujumbura and he was asking me to call and talk to her. This email was his first communication with me in six months after that first condemning email he had sent me. He was very reserved and cautious in this message. I could tell he was afraid of hurting my feelings again. He didn't know what my anger measured on the Richter magnitude scale. First, he said, "Thank you for the money you recently sent to our parents. I was able to get Mom's eyeglasses." Huh? My heart skipped a beat. *Eyeglasses for mother?* I decided to call the next day. But I was anxious about how I was going to tell my mother about my divorce. I didn't know how much information she had, or if she had even been told. So, when I spoke to her on the phone, I was also cautious. We greeted each other, and she asked me in her usual calm tone, how I was doing, and how the kids were doing. "We're doing fine, Ma," I said, "except that I have gotten divorced." I said it so quickly to get the words out before they burnt my tongue. I waited for a critical lecture, harsh words telling me how she was disappointed in me, or maybe a frantic cry. Now, you have to understand, my mother is not the crying type like I am. Despite all that she had lived through, I can barely remember any time I've seen her cry. Maybe she did in hiding; I don't know!

I was preparing for an exit sentence if she started telling me, "How could you?" But she responded in a relatively reserved, but sweet voice. "Yes, we heard about it, but the important thing is that you and the kids are all right." Wow, Mother! She didn't accuse me of being poorly raised by my grandmother who spoiled me to death, like everyone else used to tell me. I was amazed. I could feel that she was relieved to hear my voice and know that the children and I were doing fine. I decided to shift from the divorce conversation to her health. She went on to tell me that her vision was deteriorating, she had cataracts, and that the doctor had prescribed her eyeglasses.

Frankly, I couldn't picture my mom in eyeglasses with all the myriad farm and domestic chores she had to do on a daily basis. Just imagining her in nerdy big *O* eyeglasses made me want to scream. Old age was definitely catching up with her, and I wanted to stop it. Just stop it!

"Somebody needs Lasik eye surgery," I said mixing Kirundi and English as I teased her.

"What?" she asked as the phone cracked with static.

"Nothing, Ma," I said. It's not like my mother knew what Lasik surgery was. I immediately wished to be rich so I could provide her with the operation right away. Jokingly, I said to her, "Mama, you have to be careful not to drop your eyeglasses when you're cooking over the fire!" She laughed. She even understood my humor. I instantly started to know a different woman than the mother who had given birth to me. She was very confident, compassionate, asking appropriate questions, and listening to my answers. I cried silently from a mix of different emotions.

All of a sudden, I felt like a little girl who needed her mommy to make it all better. I tried to conceal my crying because I was afraid that if she knew how miserable I felt, she might get sick. But I am sure she could at least hear my sniffling, and she knew how much of a crier I was. We went on chatting about other things.

"How is Dad?" I asked.

"He's fine but getting old."

Then I surprised myself by asking her,

"Has he stopped his abusive behavior toward you?"

I held my breath as I waited for her to answer.

She laughed and said,

"Yes, he has stopped. He isn't getting any younger."

My parents had been married for more than fifty years, but I don't know how many of those years my mother was ever happy. I was so relieved to hear that my father was finally changing his behavior toward her. I was tired of this nonsense cultural tradition of abuse, where women could die in the silence of their homes, and no one would raise a finger to stop it. As a matter of fact, I had made up my mind that my next visit to Burundi would be focused on my dad's behavior. I had laid out the entire plan. Someone had to stand up for our mother's sake. She was old and frail, plus I felt that someone had to break the cycle of abuse, and I wasn't afraid to stand up to my father. All my life, I had struggled with my father's shortcomings, especially his abusive behavior toward my mother.

So, when I talked with my mom that day, I felt released from my own anger. I even felt sorry for Dad that it took him old age to change his behavior. Then, I decided that the next time I visited my family, I would show more love toward my dad. I would take a walk with him and hold his hand (fantasy here!) But even if we couldn't hold hands, I would sit with him and tell him how much I had missed his love, and how much I loved him. I would ask him to leave his children and grand-children with a good legacy of love. This talk with my mother released tremendous pressure that had built up in me. I said a prayer that night, asking for blessings for each one of my family members.

CHAPTER 16 EVOLVING QUESTIONS FOR REFLECTION

1. Describe a time when you were very unhappy in your life.

_____

_____

_____

_____

_____

2. What actions did you take to change your mindset?

_____

_____

_____

_____

_____

3. As a result of going through this adversity, what have you learned about who you are and what you stand for?

_____

_____

_____

_____

_____

Chapter 17

SEARCHING FOR GREENER PASTURES

It is only in adventure that some people succeed in knowing them-selves —in finding themselves.
—Andre Gide

In the 1920s, my grandparents on both sides moved from the highlands of Burundi's southern province of Bururi, all in search of greener pastures for their cattle in the lower lands of the current province of Makamba. Moving from one place to another has always been a way of searching for a better life. In my case, using the word migration would be an understatement. I have become an international mover. From Burundi to Québec to Ontario to Michigan to Washington, packing is just in my blood or something. Believe me, I realize how blessed I have been to get to see and live in so many beautiful places. However, after a certain age, it becomes natural for a person to want to settle down, and leave U-Haul trucks alone.

I had hoped, after buying our house in Michigan, that I was done moving. I thought that would be our permanent address. I liked our beautiful house, located in a tidy suburb where every-thing was in reach. I loved the lovely pond right in our backyard where I had watched numerous geese make out in the summer. I liked walking to the parks, sometimes with my son riding his bike, and sometimes alone. I had fantasized about my kids growing up in that house and moving out to go to college, leaving me in an empty nest, but giving them a beautiful home to come to during their Thanksgiving, Christmas, and Easter breaks.

The hardest part of moving out of that house and neighborhood was that my kids had had enough of moving. I felt that as parents, we had failed to provide them a permanent address so they could graduate without changing schools or needing to leave their friends again. I had promised them that even after the divorce, we would stay put so they wouldn't have to change schools. But with their father living so far away from them, I had to think again. Therefore, I decided to move so the kids could have access to both parents. I wasn't going to be the one who deprived my kids from seeing their father. It was up to me to make the sacrifice. The day I had to tell my kids that we would have to move once school let out, it broke my heart. They cried, they complained, they were very angry. But I was prepared to let them vent. I felt like the ultimate betrayer. This move was part of a series of losses for us. First, our marriage, second, our home, but I felt strongly about gaining a real life in being true to myself.

When my kids finally calmed down, and I was able to talk to them again, I explained as calmly as I could what had shifted. Although I wanted to protect them from having to experience moving again, my decision was based on their being close to their father so they could have a relationship with him. I didn't want them only to see him on major holidays; I wanted him to be a part of their lives as they were growing up, and they would someday move out and be on their own.

"But Mom, our friends live here!" they argued.

"I know, but we can always find friends anywhere as long as we are friends with ourselves first," I replied. They didn't buy this one, and thought I had been reading my books again.

They were still upset and depressed, but then, I unwrapped a surprise I had been keeping from them—tickets to go to Walt Disney World for a week's vacation over spring break. They jumped for joy! I knew this would come in handy. When I decided that we would move to Seattle, I saw the trip as an opportunity to buy my kids' agreement to move (A little African bribery never hurt anybody!) Not that they wouldn't have moved without the trip to Florida, but it was an incentive. I knew once we moved to the West Coast, it would be more expensive to fly to Florida. I wanted to tell them that with proper planning, any dream can come true. At that point, they finally gave me the green light.

The trip to Florida was a treat for my kids and me. I wasn't sure I could undertake it by myself, but we traveled like pros. Orlando is such a pretty, clean city, and for us coming from Michigan, very warm. March was the best time because it was not too hot yet, just comfortable weather. On the first day, we went to Downtown Disney, where we strolled the shops, and then rented a boat that Carmelle drove (I was afraid). Later, we went to watch Cirque du Soleil—what a nice spectacle! The second day, we went to our first theme park stop: Epcot. My kids vowed that they would make me go on all the rides no matter how scary they were. And I did, mostly to be there for my son, and compensate for his dad's absence.

The third day, we took a break, and the fourth day, we went to our second theme park: Disney's Hollywood Studios. Two scary rides there really got to me: Rock 'n' Roller Coaster and The Twilight Zone Tower of Terror (I still have goose bumps from that one). But again for my kids, these weren't scary; they were thrillers. I went on both rides and I made it! On the fifth day, a friend had recommended we visit the Kennedy Space Center. It was very impressive to be part of a NASA team as we took our first space shuttle, a simulated shuttle launch that leaves you in awe. We also took a tour to see the famous United States Astronaut Hall of Fame, and you can never leave without going to the IMAX films.

When we returned to our hotel that night, we were so tired, but I had a sense of accomplishment. I felt that I had beaten some demons. That I had realized this Disney vacation dream with my kids for the first time filled me with joy, even if my bank account was low. My satisfaction came from the fact that my kids could grow up knowing that they are precious, that they are worth the financial sacrifices I made, and that they can achieve whatever they want. This trip was as much my dream come true as theirs.

After the trip to Florida, I started getting in the moving mode. Some of my friends, whom I told about my decision to move after the divorce, questioned my intentions. "Why do you want to move and follow a man you divorced?" they asked. "Are you planning to reconcile?" One day, a man whose family I had befriended earlier, called me. He was someone I esteemed because of his position in the community, so I felt comfortable sharing with him and his wife about my ended marriage. The day he called me, I told him I was moving to Seattle. He said, "Seconde, I think you're making a big mistake by moving to Seattle. Why don't you stay here in Michigan?"

"I want my kids to see their father much more often than once or twice a year," I told him.

"I don't understand why your husband let you divorce him in the first place. I would never let you get away if you were my wife," he said.

"Well, I am flattered!" I said, not knowing where this conversation was going.

Then he added, "I have something to tell you."

"What is it?" I asked.

"Well, Seconde, I like you; I like you a lot, and I was thinking maybe we could go somewhere together. We could go to Florida and meet there for a vacation."

I was confused at first, not understanding what he intended. "But I just came from Florida in March with my kids; I cannot go back there again, at least not now. You should take your family; it's a really nice family vacation," I said.

"Well, no. My wife is working long hours and doesn't have time to take a vacation." Then understanding began to dawn on me.

"Sooo...this will be our vacation, just you and me?" I asked to clarify.

"Yes, just you and me...You know...we can start things slowly... no rush...no rush!" he said confidently. I was very shocked that a married man was asking me to go places alone with him. Did he think that because I was divorced, I could just run with anyone? I told him to take that energy and go home to his wife and focus on her; and I ended both the call and the friendship. I struggled with this incident for a couple of days after. How could he? If his wife were indeed working too much to have a relationship with her husband as he claimed (if that were even true), how would an affair have resolved their problems? Did he want a friendship with benefits? Anyway, that was my reentrance into singlehood. I don't remember where I heard that men are not good at being friends with the opposite sex unless they're gay. Is that really true? Well, that could be a subject for another book.

In June of 2008, my kids and I landed in the evergreen state. It was my first time going to Seattle. Although I had some anticipation as I always do when I visit a new place, I didn't know what to expect. I just hoped for the best. I had only heard positive things about Seattle from people who had been there or who lived there. I didn't know if the highly boasted job market I had heard about would apply to me. I didn't know what to expect about people; were they friendly or not? And I knew it was a rainy city.

A month later, as I unpacked our belongings in the 1,200 square foot rented apartment, I realized what a drop in lifestyle the move had meant. I was moving from a 2,500 square foot home into a place less than half its size. Life really has a funny way of turning. But I didn't feel sad. Although my kids complained about the small space, I let them complain all they wanted. This was all I could afford with my child support income. I had yet to settle down and find a job. To look on the bright side, I told my kids that at least our cleaning chores would be cut in half as well. I would not have to shovel the snow in winters, or do all the men's work I was doing in my home in Michigan, which would decrease my stress.

I knew I would miss the privacy of living in my own home, but I was being "born again" by turning bad into good. At the tender age of forty-one, a time when I should have been reaping the stable life for which I thought I had sacrificed, I found myself in a divorce court explaining why I mattered in sharing my marital assets. The house I thought I had worked for, and deserved more than anyone, was taken away. What else could I have done other than accept the situation? I had lived a seemingly good life, but underneath I had been so depleted. Therefore, the drop in square footage didn't seem so threatening to me, because I was gaining my sanity. If I were no longer compromising my values, I could live with the shrinkage in space.

Now that I was living in the same vicinity with my ex-husband, I crafted a parenting schedule that respected his working hours and gave the kids time to see him. The weekends seemed to be working better for all concerned. The kids agreed with the schedule because they could only bring a few things with them on weekends at their dad's and live with me for the rest of the week. The first time they went to spend the night at their father's apartment, I was a wreck. Although I had anticipated some deserved "me" time and was certainly looking forward to the solitude; once they left, the quietness became nerve-wracking. I had to put the television at high volume to block out the outside noise and the inside quietness. When it was time to go to bed, I have to admit, I was a little scared. I felt that my kids had been my security guards. They provided me with assurance that I was never alone during the night; they shielded me from too much quietness.

The TV remote control that belonged to my son exclusively, now that he was gone, I held on to it as if it were a life preserver. The shows I had always wanted to watch but couldn't because they seemed inappropriate for my son to see, no longer had any appeal. I told myself, "Welcome to Divorcée Land, Mademoiselle. What did you think it would be like?" But, I had no choice but to get used to this new routine. As the days of this new living arrangement rolled on, I started to feel safer in my apartment when the kids were at their father's house.

The first time the kids asked me what I did on the weekend while they were gone, I just said, "Oh, I had fun!" not wanting to tell them I was a wreck.

"Fun…? You had fun? What about us? We don't get to have any fun; you get rid of us so you can have fun?" Hearing them say that tore at my heart. I wanted to tell them, "Okay, sweeties, you can stay with me if you don't want to visit your dad." But instead I said, "Look at it this way; you have two parents who love you very much. There is no reason you shouldn't see both. Now we don't live in the same household anymore, but you guys need to be cared for by both of us, okay?" There was no turning back, and I told them that they should enjoy the time spent with their father because that was the reason we had moved from Michigan, so they could see him more often. I also told them that some kids do not get the chance to see their father at all, which affects them their whole lives.

"But Dad is not even home when we're at his house," they pleaded with me.

"Sweetie, I cannot be Mom and Dad," I finally lashed out. "Your dad needs to make adjustments and make sure he is there for you."

"I hate my life!" said my outspoken, teenage-daughter Elva.

The kids are the ones who get the worst of it in a divorce, no doubt about it. Parents can always rebuild their lives, but kids have a tough time transitioning. After we talked about this "getting rid of them" incident, the kids started to accept the situation. I did my best to be present whenever they were with me, and I stopped bullying myself into thinking I wasn't a good mother just because I lacked financial resources. I realized I gave them more than money could buy. I gave them a feeling of safety, someone solid to rely on, and most times at my own expense.

Kids are also resilient. They sense it when a parent tries for their sake, and they appreciate it even though it's hard for them to express. Elva doesn't know this, but I read one of her essays she wrote for school when she was a high school freshman. She wrote, "The year 2008 was hard for my mom. First she got divorced, and now she hasn't been able to find a new job. She had a tough time, but she is a maverick!" That warmed my heart to know that my daughter appreciated my trials in life, and saw them as triumphs.

Elva's sister, Carmelle, on the other hand, is much more reserved. As I write this, she is at a cross-road between adolescence and adulthood. She is trying to figure out what she wants to do when she grows up. When she was younger, she wanted to be a kids' doctor. Now she has changed her mind, but she is still interested in working with kids some day. She says she would like to help out in Africa, and she wants to volunteer with some orphanages in Rwanda and Burundi after she graduates from college. I encourage her to follow her heart and choose whatever will make her happy.

As for Darrel, he is my little prince. The girls say that he is my favorite child, but of course, it's not true! That's because he is our only son and youngest child, so I guess he gets the best of both worlds. The girls themselves spoiled him more than I did when he was younger. Sometimes, when I want Darrel to help me with something, let's say, take the garbage out, I say to him, "Darrel, sweetie, you know what? You're the best son I've ever had! Can you take the garbage out for me?"

He replies, "Mom, I'm your only son!" Then he turns the trick around and says,

"Mom, since I'm your only son, can you take the garbage out for your only son, please? Thank you, Mom!" We ping pong this for a few minutes, and then he takes the garbage out. I am very fortunate to have these three kids in my life—these beautiful angels God blessed me with.

CHAPTER 17 EVOLVING QUESTIONS FOR REFLECTION

1. Do you consider yourself an adventurer?

_____

_____

_____

_____

2. If so, in what area?

_____

_____

_____

_____

3. What have you learned about your adventurous self?

_____

_____

_____

_____

Chapter 18

CELEBRATING MOMENTS OF BLISS

Life isn't a matter of milestones, but of moments.
—Rose Kennedy

Although I could be complaining that life isn't fair, gas prices are high, blah, blah, blah…I've chosen to be content with the present. I've chosen to stop blaming myself for what I have failed to do in the past, and I am enjoying everyday life with little things such as a walk in the neighborhood, going up and down the hills, breathing fresh air (which is what I called "fun" when my kids asked me what I did on weekends). I've learned to start celebrating moments in my life, because life is just that—moments. I celebrate who I am in this moment. I started treating myself to nice getaways and going to nice places like when I went to Vancouver, British Columbia. Let it be no secret, I love to travel! Especially when I'm feeling down, a trip to some place new reenergizes me.

That's what I did one day when I took the Greyhound bus to Vancouver, a year after I had been living in Washington State. It was the last weekend of September, and that meant the warm weather would not last any longer. In Seattle as in Vancouver, October is a raining month, and the following months, and all winter long. That day, it was neither too hot, nor too cold—just the right weather. After I got off the bus, I was welcomed by a beautiful sunny 70 degrees Fahrenheit as I exited the Greyhound station. I felt like kissing the ground, I was so happy. After browsing around Yale-town in downtown Vancouver, I walked to my hotel room. The sun kept me company, I could feel it warming up my back and my behind. The gentle breeze penetrated and moved around my braids I had cut short; I was afraid it showed the spots where the braids had already come off. Then I realized I was in a new city where no one knew me. They could not tell if my braids were old or new. I wore my "You never know what the weather is gonna be" outfit—cute jeans with a matching jacket, and a short sleeve V-neck shirt. I love this outfit to this day whenever I travel; it keeps me warm without burning me. I was also wearing my not too high or too low brown sandals. They were easy to walk with. And off I went and melted into the walking crowd, and before I knew it, I was at the hotel where I had reserved a room for one night. Just for me! This was really a new me. Indulging in a cozy hotel and all!

After I put my few belongings in the room, my stomach started growling. It was about 3:30 p.m., and I had only had the breakfast I had brought on the bus that morning. I went to the lobby and asked the receptionist if there were any restaurants in the walking vicinity since I had no car. I didn't mind walking; walking in big cities provides me with an opportunity to observe the walking crowd. I ask myself, "Where are those people from? How long are they here for?" Well, I was there only for the day so I might as well enjoy it. The hotel receptionist offered to give me a map with all the restaurants and other things to do in Vancouver, but I declined. "No thanks, I don't do maps!" I said. "I can read written instructions, but no map, please. I'm not a map person." She smiled and gave me five names of different types of restaurants. Then she said,

"It really depends on what kind of food you like." I scanned my brain for any favorite food, but nothing came to mind.

"I like all kinds of food; that's the trouble," I said. This time, she laughed out loud, but she managed to keep it professional.

Then she added, "There is also a good Japanese restaurant that makes good sushi, and there is an Indian restaurant a couple of blocks from here."

"That's it! God, I am craving Indian food!" I said, and without any further delay, I asked her to give me the address to the Indian restaurant; I almost ran to get there. I was already drooling at the excitement of Indian spices; I smelled curry all over while going to the restaurant. It took me a while to find, but I finally let myself in as if I owned the place. It was about 4:20 p.m., and it wasn't dinner time quite yet, so I was lucky it wasn't busy. When the waiter gave me the menu, I ordered a glass of red merlot (my usual whenever I take wine), and for food he advised charbroiled salmon. When the food came, it was sizzling! Have you ever eaten sizzling salmon? Let me tell you, if you're a fan of fish, it is mouth-watering. Pieces of salmon mixed with red onions, herbs, green and red peppers, a mix of curry, and other Indian spices I couldn't identify, and rice for a side dish. I said grace and thanked the Lord for this feast I was about to devour (emphasis on devour). But the prayer was inter-rupted by my first bite—I was starving.

Half-way done, I slowed down and reflected on how lucky I was to be enjoying this beautiful city, delicious food, and nice weather. It didn't get any better than this. Then I meditated on where I came from, how much I missed my family in Burundi, and I was about to turn this feast into guilt, but then I stopped myself, "No non-sense again, Seconde, you are worthy of this; remember, you're learning to value yourself." So, I deleted the thought. Little by little, I was learning that it was okay for me to take a break, to breathe without guilt.

On my way back to the hotel, the sun was still out, but almost waving goodbye on the horizon. As I passed crowds, I saw a homeless person with his paper cup, and I feigned paying no attention as I wondered how such a beautiful and vibrant city had homeless, too. A yard farther, I saw another homeless man, and this one struck me because of his youth. He was a young man maybe in his late twenties; he was sitting on the floor and had his hat on the floor, upside down for people to put cash in. But people kept passing without paying any attention to him. I passed as well. A couple of steps away, I saw yet another homeless person—this time a woman sprawled on the sidewalk. I almost gave her money by impulse, just because she was a woman. But, I didn't want to encourage her to keep begging on the streets. But then, a voice in my head told me that the $4.75 Canadian money I had in my pocket would not serve me much once I went back to Seattle the next day. I stepped backwards and almost knocked down the person behind me. I bent as much as I could to reach the homeless woman's paper cup, and I dropped in the two toonies (that's what Canadians called their two dollar coins) and three quarters I had. The coins made a prrr…noise in her cup. She said, "Thank you." I said, "You're welcome," and I continued my way. As I was approaching the hotel, a thought came to me, "God what have I done? I am encouraging that woman to stay on the streets and beg instead of staying home. What if she buys drugs with my money? I don't want any part of that! Is that good giving or bad giving?" But instead of feeling guilty, I felt blissful (probably the Indian spices were kicking in). I realized God was filling my own cup, so I could fill someone else's. Whatever circumstances made her end up on the streets, shouldn't prevent me from doing good. Once we give, we should give unconditionally, and we have no control over what the person will use the money for. I could only hope it was for good, not self-destruction.

That day, I learned that taking time for me to refuel and reenergize without guilt (still a work in progress) is paramount. I had to learn that taking care of me doesn't mean abandoning anyone, as it had been ingrained in my psyche. When I do something for someone else, I don't feel any guilt. For instance, when I send financial support to my family in Burundi, I don't feel any guilt; when I help out a cousin here or a niece there, I feel no guilt. But why is it that if I do something solely for me, I freak out? That's because I never learned to value myself enough to think that I'm worthy of good things. I didn't have a role model in that area. All the women in my life labored from dawn to sunset and never took care of themselves. My evolvement might have taken a long time, but I know I am honoring my true self one day at a time. As the wise Ralph Waldo Emerson said, "Life is a journey, not a destination…"

CHAPTER 18 EVOLVING QUESTIONS FOR REFLECTION

1. Was there a time in your life when you felt unworthy of anything? What caused the feelings, and what were your emotions at that time?

_____

_____

_____

_____

_____

2. How did you deal with the feelings and/or emotions? Did you change anything in your circumstances? How, and what were the results?

_____

_____

_____

_____

_____

3. As a result of the changes you made, what did you learn that could help others in a similar situation?

_____

_____

_____

_____

_____

Chapter 19

FORGIVING

You will know that forgiveness has begun when you recall those who
hurt you and feel the power to wish them well.
—Lewis B. Smedes

"What therefore God has joined together, let not man put asunder" (Mark 10:9). Our pastor quoted this scripture before asking for the rings, which my son Darrel had been guarding carefully in the pocket of his suit. It was Easter Sunday of 2013, and our wedding took place in a small church my husband had been attending since our divorce five years before. This church had changed him in so many ways. There couldn't have been any better fitting day for us, as we rededicated ourselves to loving each other until death do us apart. Our marriage was resurrected, just as Jesus had resurrected from the dead; and hence, we chose to get married on Easter Day.

Before our marriage was restored, it had been dead for many years. It had been eroded of its many ingredients: trust, respect, honesty, affection, and I had never thought it could be restored.

You see, my ex-husband and I had been apart for five years and legally divorced for four. Although many of our friends and relatives always told me that we would, could, and should reconcile, I had given up on this relationship. I had been hurt enough to finally call it quits five years earlier. Anyone who suggested that I go back either didn't know anything about what I had gone through, or was just plain cruel. And it's not like my ex-husband hadn't tried to get me back. Claver had never wanted the divorce in the first place, but he also lived in denial of the mistakes he had made as the head of our family, mistakes that had contributed to our divorce. I didn't want to get back with someone who wouldn't acknowledge his mistakes. As humans, we all make mistakes, and I had my share, but admitting and learning from them is the first step toward making things better, especially in relationships. Although he wasn't the source of all my miseries, Claver had contributed to igniting them during our marriage. And his unwillingness to work on our marital issues had contributed to the divorce, no matter who filed; it takes two to tango. I'm sure I had ignited some of his miseries as well. We both had our issues to work on in order to become the people God created us to be. I'm not suggesting divorce is the best way to work on a marriage; everyone's path is different. But it was the way our destiny was mapped out for that particular time in our lives.

So for a long time, I was certain getting back together would never happen. But Claver wouldn't leave me alone. Eventually, we came to a point where he acknowledged the mistakes he had made as a husband, and he apologized about them. He had become a converted Christian and was involved in his church. He had requested prayers, asking God to reconcile our marriage. But, we had been divorced for a reason—many reasons for that matter, and I couldn't feel in my heart of hearts that he had changed. It took a lot of praying, and waiting on God's timetable to be able to forgive my ex-husband and even think about reconciling.

Claver continued to ask me whether I would give him another chance, so he could show me how much he had changed or grown as a person. He would send me flowers through our kids or just bring them to my apartment. He gave me more flowers while we were divorced than during the sixteen years we were married. On Mother's Day, he would take me and the kids for brunch, hoping that I would consider getting back together with him. I had been disappointed in so many ways that I just couldn't consider it. At one point, I was getting worn out by his insistent pursuit, so I changed my prayers. Instead of asking God to send me a tall, dark, and handsome man, I asked God to help me forgive my ex-husband.

Then one day, it dawned on me that there was no way I could forgive my ex-husband, without forgiving my father for what he had done or not done for me, my mother, and my siblings. I felt held in captivity by my father's sins, and I needed to rid myself of them. Slowly, I was coming to an understanding of myself, and a realization that to have a real relationship with any man, I first had to let go of the first man whom I considered had failed me—my dad. He and I had some unfinished business, and I couldn't go on with my life, while carrying this load. I needed closure. And the way I wanted to carry out this plan was to show more love to my father than ever before. He and my mother were close to eighty years of age, and to be frank, they had led their lives. Bad or good, who was I to judge at this point in their lives? I wanted to let my parents know that whatever life they still had to live, I would be there for them and help them as I was already doing, the best way I could. I am a grown woman now, and my parents needed me more than I needed them. It's the circle of life, and I decided I couldn't be out of shape forever because I had missed my parents' love as a child. I knew they had loved me the best they could, provided their life circumstances. I couldn't hold them responsible for my

life experiences even if they had influenced it in many ways. I had
to accept them for who they are. And I wanted to tell them that,
and free myself from any bondage.

In the summer of 2012, I made up my mind, took a month off
work, and booked airfare tickets for my daughter Elva and me.
Elva had just graduated from high school, and our trip was her
graduation gift in a sense. We joined Carmelle, who was already
in Rwanda for her college study abroad program with her school.
After Carmelle finished her program, the girls and I spent a week
in Kigali, and we had a lot of fun. We discovered *"le pays des milles
collines"* ("the country of one thousand hills"). It was a chance for
my daughters to learn about the Rwandans' recent history; we visited the genocide memorial and other sites. We saw how much the
country had changed since the atrocities of 1994, and how fast it
was rebuilding.

After seven days in Kigali, we crossed the southern border to
Burundi by bus. In Burundi, my daughters and I enjoyed the warm
weather and the welcome of family and friends. Many had not seen
my kids in as many as fifteen years. We took every opportunity
to go to the beaches at Lake Tanganyika. We visited family and
friends spread out all over the country. And I had a chance to visit
Uncle Apollinaire who had paid for my elementary school. I hadn't
seen him in more than twenty years. Unfortunately, his health had
deteriorated due to a head injury; he couldn't even recognize me,
which saddened me so much. I wanted to thank him for what he
had done for me, but I could only share the joy with his family. He
was unaware of my visit, but nonetheless, we danced, and praised
him, hoping that at least his spirit could share in the festivities with
us.

The visit to my parents couldn't have been more timely.
Sometimes, we feel a nudge, urging us to do something; and some-

times, we ignore or dismiss it. But the nudge I felt urging me to go to Burundi in 2012 really helped me say goodbye to my father. You see, I had travelled to Burundi to make peace with myself and those I love—to sever my wounds linked to my upbringing, a figurative way of cutting the umbilical cord that still bonded me to my parents. As my daughters and I visited my parents in my hometown of Vugizo, we were accompanied by my nieces and nephew, Cyriaque's children, as well as his wife Judith. We had fun, and spent three days visiting and enjoying my family and my many relatives. I noticed how old my father had become, but compared to my mother, he still looked pretty good. Mom was frail, and as I said my goodbyes to them the last day of our visit, I cried as I hugged my parents. I felt sadness, but I wasn't entirely sure why I was crying. But again, I'm a crier, so no one seemed surprised anymore. And when I cried, my daughters cried as well, and everyone around me cried, my goodness! But I was also relieved for having come this far with my daughters to see their grandparents. Carmelle had been five years old, and Elva two, the last time they had seen my family. It was an overdue visit. Even for me, it had been six years since I had visited with my son Darrel. In all, this was a wonderful trip.

The very same night we got back to Seattle from Burundi, I received a call from my sister-in-law Judith. She told me that my dad had passed away the same night I was traveling back. He got sick, threw up blood, and was gone on the same day. No one knew what caused it since the family didn't get a chance to take him to the hospital. But we suspected it was a case of stomach hemorrhaging since Dad had undergone an ulcer operation twenty five years earlier. He had started feeling stomach pain in recent years, but nothing dramatic, so his sudden death was a surprise to everyone. To be honest, I thought Mom would be the first to go because she looked so frail. I wasn't sure I would see her again. Now, she is a widow, and I don't know how long she still has on this Earth, and as I write this book, I certainly hope she will live long enough to see it published and read it. Yeah, maybe when it's translated into Latin, the only foreign language she read when she was a young girl in catechism school in the 1940s.

A week after my father's passing, I had a dream. In the dream, Dad appeared to be talking to me in an animated way. I couldn't see his whole body, only from the neck up. He seemed happy, laughed, and I laughed along. I was reminded of his early days when he would crack jokes on good days when he would come home happy, and no one would get hurt. He would tell us many anecdotes of his early days in East Africa, and we would laugh. That was the time I always enjoyed being in my father's presence. So, in this dream he was telling me some of those jokes, no doubt, and we both laughed and enjoyed the conversation. Like in any dream, you want it to last, especially if it's a good one. You want to know more, remember more after the dream, but I'm surprised I even recall all this. I usually forget all my dreams the minute I wake up. But this dream stuck and I made sure I wrote it down the next day because I wanted to try and understand it.

Now I don't pretend to know how to interpret dreams, but for my sanity, I took it to mean that somewhere, somehow, my father was proud of me. In his living days, Dad had never told me that he was proud of me or that he loved me. But, we also never crossed each other. I always made sure I stayed away as much as possible, and like I said in a previous chapter, Dad took this behavior as me being the sweet child. Maybe I was daddy's little girl after all? Hey, I said it was a dream! But whatever the dream was meant to tell me, I also took it as a sign to move on with my life, and not to carry my father's burden—to open up to love again, and to bless someone with my love.

It was exactly during this time that my relationship with my ex-husband improved exponentially, and that I decided to forgive him and give him another chance. We dated for about three months, and he bought an engagement ring and proposed in front of the kids on Christmas Eve of 2012. Three months later, we got married at the church he had been attending since our divorce, where he had requested prayers for our reconciliation. The whole congregation pitched in and helped us prepare the wedding. This wedding was on a tight budget, but I made sure we had a wedding cake this time, and our daughter Carmelle helped pay for it; thank you, sweetie. Uh…no, there were no fruit cups, okay!

We said our testimonies, and mine was about forgiving my husband, forgiving myself, and forgiving others, letting go, and letting God. Our song was "Wind Beneath My Wings" sung by Bette Midler (I love that song). Our honeymoon was in Maui, and it was my first time going to Hawaii. I was surprised by some of its similarities with Burundi's beautiful landscape.

My husband and I had now both come full circle, and it was a wonderful time in our family.

CHAPTER 19 EVOLVING QUESTIONS FOR REFLECTION

1. Do you have someone or something from your past that you have never been able to forgive?

_____

_____

_____

_____

_____

2. If so, what do you need to do to change the situation in order to forgive and let go?

_____

_____

_____

_____

_____

3. If you have already forgiven, what was the outcome for you after you decided to forgive?

_____

_____

_____

_____

_____

DISCOVERING YOUR INNER JOY

Don't die with your music still inside you. Listen to your intuitive inner voice and find what passion stirs your soul.
—Wayne Dyer

Whatever I have attracted as life experiences from the moment I was born to this day, is an emanation from God to free me from self-slavery. I am grateful for all of it. Those circumstances were God-sent to teach me how to be self-reliant and free me from guilt, regrets, shame, and self-pity, and to teach me how to love and honor myself so I could love and honor others.

It has been a rewarding experience writing this book as I explored my own person on this life journey. Every person has a story, and only you can tell your own story. The important thing is not in what language you tell your story; that's why they invented translators. It's much more about the compelling message. I could have written this book in French, in Kirundi, or had it translated into any other language; it wouldn't have made any difference as long as the reader was fluent in the language in which the book was written.

So, what's your story? The good thing about life is that there is always something new to learn, about ourselves or others. Even if you had a perfect childhood, or perfect parents, at one point or another, life will throw you a curveball, and you will have to cope.

I believe that we face obstacles and challenges because they are God's way of helping us to rise higher, to serve our purpose in life, and to adhere to our true calling. Often times, the challenge is: How do you find the higher calling that awaits you? When you know what your purpose in life is, you are half-way to achieving it.

What is that thing you do that makes you lose track of time, and you cannot get enough of doing it? Stay with me here. I'm talking about work that you do that never feels like work. Deepak Chopra calls it "Dharma," a Sanskrit word for "purpose in life," in his book, *The Seven Spiritual Laws of Success: A Practical Guide to the Fulfillment of Your Dreams*. Such a great book.

So, my challenge to you today is: Find your passion. As in Dr. Dyer's above quote, don't die with your music still inside of you—share your gifts with the world.

Below are eighteen lessons I wish my mother had taught me before sending me out into the world. Make the list even longer by adding your own lessons learned, or ones you wish you had been taught.

18 LESSONS I WISH MY MOTHER HAD TAUGHT ME

1. **Owning your own happiness**: Do not fall into the trap of thinking that someone else is responsible for making you happy; others can contribute to making you happier, but you have to own your happiness first.

2. **Loving from within**: You cannot give what you don't have. It is by loving yourself that you can begin to love others.

3. **Getting a good education**: Nothing can substitute for a good education; it opens doors for you to use your God-given talents.

4. **Carving out financial stability**: Buy assets if you can afford to, or save money until you are clear what kind of assets you want to acquire. Invest in your retirement fund before and after you get married. If you get married and have to stay home to take care of your children and family, ask your spouse to set up a savings account in your name, and save every month. Please understand that this account is not to pay you for taking care of your family. No one can ever pay you enough for parenthood. This account is to allow you to buy underwear without having to ask for permission.

5. **Attracting the one**: Stay away from relationships that are abusive in any manner: verbal, physical, or emotional. When dating, spend some time getting to know each other before merging your lives. It is godly to choose a partner who is nice to you. Role-play your marriage before you are married to see how you and your future spouse will respond to real life circumstances. Analyze how as a couple you complement each other's personality traits. Be yourself and don't play a character, falling into the trap of unleashing the real you after your "I do's". Give each other a chance to know who you are as a person from the start.

6. **Knowing yourself**: Know what you value in a relationship. If the relationship is built on things that you value such as honesty, trust, and respect, it won't take too much "remodeling," only simple adjustments.

7. **Envisioning your future**: Envision your future with the kind of person you want to spend your life with. Experts advise that you jot down a list of qualities you want in a mate, just to be clear so you won't cheat yourself in what you value.

8. **Discussing your offspring**: How many babies do you want? Plan before you bring them into the world. Spend at least the first year having fun with your spouse (It's okay you know!) Discuss the idea of babies and how many. When he was seven years old, my son Darrel told me that he wanted to have twenty children when he gets to be a dad. At nine years old, he downsized the number to twelve because he realized that children are hard work! Joking aside, I love my children, and I would still have three children if I were to start over, but I wish somebody had told me it was okay to wait or plan before having kids.

9. **Running your own race**: Don't stand in your own way by comparing yourself to others, or being jealous of others, or unnecessarily competitive (competition has its place, but don't obsess). Otherwise, you'll run into exhaustion before you reach your own goals. Know that there will always be somebody better than you and somebody worse than you. Honor who you are by being the best *you* that you can be, right where you are.

10. **Balancing your act**: Thrive to live a physically, emotionally, and spiritually balanced life.

11. **Connecting beyond the four walls**: Humanity is intertwined; there are no "others" without the "self," and there is no "self"

without the "others." We all matter, and we have a purpose to fulfill. But, we can't do it alone.

12. **Forgiving is for yourself**: When you forgive, it's not to condone evil deeds, but for your sake, forgive to let go of resentment and negativity, to have inner peace and joy. Let God fight your battles.

13. **Seeking inner peace**: Strive to be happy rather than right.

14. **Teaching people how to treat you**: Essentially by treating others with respect, love, kindness, and compassion, you allow your spirit to open up to deeper connections, and attract likes into your life. Apply Eleanor Roosevelt's quote: "No one can make you feel inferior without your consent."

15. **Living in the moment**: Don't concern yourself with too much of tomorrow's matters. Enjoy today because it is all you know for sure. Whenever I'm having a hard time with something, I think about this phrase that helps me lighten up: "This too shall pass."

16. **Choosing your battles**: Not everything in life needs to take your energy, whether physical or emotional. Don't sweat the small stuff.

17. **Traveling for fun**: Go somewhere you've never been. I love traveling and discovering new places. For me, traveling is part of how I want to live a balanced and fulfilling life. It allows me to see how other people live, and what I can learn from them. Go see God's beautiful wonders and creations.

18. **Honoring thyself**: Apply the above lessons, and add your own lessons learned from your own life or the lives of others.

RRU MODEL — REFLECT

RRU MODEL — RECTIFY

RRU MODEL — UNITE

ACKNOWLEDGMENTS

Gratitude makes sense of our past, brings peace for today, and creates a vision for tomorrow.
—Melody Beattie

No one can ever succeed by doing it all alone; we all need each other. So the following are people who helped me in achieving my goal of writing this book, and to them, I express my heartfelt gratitude. My thanks go to:

My writing instructor, Nick O'Connell in Seattle, you got the first glimpses of my writing ambitions in the summer of 2008 and encouraged me to keep it up.

My writing buddies in Nick's class: Lyn, Susan, and Kris, you made me feel less "alien," and I thank you for your kind encouragement, especially during the book's early drafts.

Nancy Wick, for your hard work editing my first draft, your keen eye for details was very helpful.

Patrick Snow, my publishing coach. Patrick, you do more than help publish books, or build businesses; you help people achieve their dreams. Thank you Coach!

My editor, Tyler Tichelaar, for your hard work editing this book and helping me put on the finishing touches.

Susan Friedmann of AVIVA Publishing, for welcoming me to the AVIVA family.

Shiloh Schroeder of Fusion Creative Works, and everyone who has touched this book in one way or another during its publishing process.

ABOUT THE AUTHOR

Originally from Burundi, Central Africa, Seconde Nimenya travelled in 1992 for the first time outside her native land to Québec, Canada, joining her husband Claver who was pursuing his education. In 1993, they were planning to return to Burundi when a civil war broke out and all hope of ever returning to her beloved country was shattered.

Seconde holds a bachelor's degree in Human Arts and Sciences from the University of Burundi with a history major. In Canada, she graduated with a bachelor's degree in business administration with a major in finance from the University of Sherbrooke in Québec. After living in Canada for twelve years, she and her family moved to Michigan, as she furthered her education, and received an MBA from the University of Phoenix in 2005.

In Canada and in the U.S., she was involved in different organizations that promote equal opportunities, improve the life conditions, especially for minorities, immigrants, women, and children. Seconde also is a firm believer that peace starts at home by banishing violence and abuse in all its forms.

Seconde discovered she had a gift for writing and speaking in March of 2003 when she initiated the celebration of International Women's Day in Windsor, Canada, and was the main speaker in both French and English. She loves reading and writing, and she has received honorable mention for some of her nonfiction stories. She speaks and writes fluently three languages: Kirundi, French, and English. Seconde has lived on two continents and in three different countries, and has travelled to many lovely places. As a result, she has written this book to inspire and encourage you to discover and honor your true self.

ABOUT THE NISE GROUP

The NISE Group is a sole proprietorship founded by Author Seconde Nimenya. It encompasses her services she provides as an author, an inspirational Speaker, as well as a leadership Mentor through her RRU Model to inspire personal growth. RRU stands for Reflect- Rectify- Unite. Through this unique model, Seconde Nimenya coaches and mentors others to rise above their obstacles, discover their passion, and honor their true self.

The NISE Group's mission is to inspire people worldwide to overcome adversities, discover who they are, find their passion, achieve positive change, and honor themselves. The NISE Group focuses its energy in the following areas:

Author: This book is available on the website:

www.EvolvingThroughAdversity.com

Retailers such as bookstores or online retailers can purchase Seconde Nimenya's book and other products at a special wholesale discount.

Speaker: Seconde will tailor her messages to the needs of your audiences.

Evolving Coach: Seconde can be booked as an Evolving Coach with your organization or group, to coach your audience in regards to finding their passion and be leaders in their own lives.

www.SecondeNimenya.com

www.ReflectRectifyUnite.com

Please visit the company website at: **www.TheNiseGroup.com**

BOOK SECONDE NIMENYA
TO SPEAK AT YOUR NEXT EVENT

Seconde Nimenya has a passion in helping others overcome obstacles, and honor themselves. Through her unique leadership and positive change model, the RRU Model or Reflect-Rectify-Unite Model, Seconde Nimenya has inspired others in her prior involvement in various nonprofit organizations both in Canada, and the United States of America.

Whether your audience is a couple of people or thousands, Seconde Nimenya can deliver a customized message of inspiration. As an immigrant who has had to overcome adversities in her native country and adjust to another culture once in North America, Seconde will approach your audience with humor, and will entertain and inspire them in a way that will leave them wanting more.

You can contact Seconde Nimenya by phone at: 425-213-8606 or By email at: nisecond@gmail.com or seconde@ EvolvingThroughAdversity.com